OLD MOORE'S

HOROSCOPE AND ASTRAL DIARY

PISCES

OLD MOORE'S

HOROSCOPE AND ASTRAL DIARY

PISCES

foulsham
LONDON • NEW YORK • TORONTO • SYDNEY

foulsham

The Publishing House, Bennetts Close,
Cippenham, Slough, Berks SL1 5AP, England

Foulsham books can be found in all good bookshops or direct from
www.foulsham.com

ISBN: 978-0-572-03461-0

A CIP record for this book is available from the British Library

Printed in Great Britain by Creative Print and Design Wales, Blaina.

CONTENTS

INTRODUCTION

Welcome to Old Moore's Astral Diaries for the year 2009. Old Moore has been searching the skies on your behalf for centuries now, and the timeless truths of astrology are as relevant to the lives of millions of people today as they ever were. Modern astrology is not seen as a case of each of us waiting around for the forces of the universe to drop good or bad fortune into our laps. On the contrary, it is a complex series of generally subtle changes that have more to do with the way we look at the world and react to it. Astrology gives us an opportunity to make the very best of whatever cosmological forces are acting upon us at any point in time

It is in an effort to harness and use these forces in a positive way that Old Moore has created the Astral Diary for 2009 – a complete book geared specifically towards you and the influences that help to make you what you are.

If you want to know whether a new romance is likely to blossom, if you are in for a good time on the money front or if family concerns could be making you less positive than you might usually be – Old Moore is here to help. The Astral Diary allows you an easy-to-follow, daily account of the way the stars and planets are having a bearing on your life and also lets you know how you can maximise your potential. In addition, the diaries offer space for you to add your own notes and comments.

Old Moore does much more than looking at your zodiac sign because the Astral Diaries let you look much deeper into your own individual nature. What you are as a person is reflected in the time of day you were born and by the position of certain heavenly bodies such as the Moon and the planet Venus. Using unique tables in the Astral Diary you can work out exactly why you are what you are in very specific ways. Once you have this information you can then deal much more effectively with the intricacies of life and will know how to react to both good and not so favourable trends.

Everything you are as an individual is captured within your astrological profile. Using the Astral Diary you can get so close to the core of planetary influence that you can almost feel the subtle undertones that, in the end, have a profound bearing on your life and circumstances. Used in the right way, astrology allows you to maximise your potential, to strike whilst the iron is hot and to live a more contented and successful life. Consulting *Old Moore's Astral Diary* will make you more aware of what really makes you tick and is a fascinating way to register the very heartbeat of the solar system of which we are all a part.

Old Moore extends his customary greeting to all people of the Earth and offers his age-old wishes for a happy and prosperous period ahead.

THE ESSENCE
OF PISCES

Exploring the Personality of Pisces the Fishes

(20TH FEBRUARY–20TH MARCH)

What's in a sign?

Pisceans are fascinating people – everyone you come across is likely to admit that fact. By nature you are kind, loving, trustful and inclined to work very hard on behalf of the people you love – and perhaps even those you don't like very much. Your nature is sympathetic and you will do anything you can to improve the lot of those you consider to be worse off than yourself. There is a very forgiving side to your temperament and also a strong artistic flair that can find an outlet in any one of a dozen different ways.

It's true you are difficult to know, and there is a very important reason for this. Your nature goes deep, so deep in fact that someone would have to live with you for a lifetime to plumb even a part of its fathomless depths. What the world sees is only ever a small part of the total magic of this most compulsive and fascinating zodiac sign. Much of your latent power and natural magic is constantly kept bottled up, because it is never your desire to manipulate those around you. Rather, you tend to wait in the shadows until opportunities to come into your own present themselves.

In love you are ardent and sincere, though sometimes inclined to choose a partner too readily and too early. There's a dreamy quality to your nature that makes you easy to adore, but which can also cause difficulties if the practical necessities of life take a very definite second place.

The chances are that you love music and picturesque scenery, and you may also exhibit a definite fondness for animals. You prefer to live in the country rather than in the middle of a noisy and smelly town, and tend to keep a reasonably well-ordered household. Your family can easily become your life and you always need a focus for your energies. You are not at all good at feathering your own nest, unless you know that someone else is also going to benefit on the way. A little more selfishness probably would not go amiss on occasions because you are often far too willing to put yourself out wholesale for people who don't respect your sacrifices. Pisceans can be full of raging passions and are some of the most misunderstood people to be found anywhere within the great circle of the zodiac.

Pisces resources

It is the very essence of your zodiac sign that you are probably sitting there and saying to yourself 'Resources? I have no resources'. Of course you are wrong, though it has to be admitted that a glaring self-confidence isn't likely to be listed amongst them. You are, however, a very deep thinker, and this can turn out to be a great advantage and a useful tool when it comes to getting on in life. Because your natural intuition is so strong (some people would call you psychic), you are rarely fooled by the glib words of others. Your own natural tendency to tell the truth can be a distinct advantage and a great help to you when it comes to getting on in life from a practical and financial viewpoint.

Whilst many of the signs of the zodiac tend to respond to life in an impulsive way, you are more likely to weigh up the pros and cons of any given situation very carefully. This means that when you do take action you can achieve much more success – as well as saving a good deal of energy on the way. People tend to confide in you automatically, so you are definitely at an advantage when it comes to knowing what makes your family and friends tick. At work you can labour quietly and confidently, either on your own or in the company of others. Some people would assert that Pisceans are model employees because you really do not know how to give anything less than your best.

Never underestimate the power of your instincts. Under most circumstances you are aware of the possible outcome of any given situation and should react as your inner mind dictates. Following this course inevitably puts you ahead of the game and explains why so quiet a sign can promote so many winners in life. Not that you are particularly competitive. It's much more important for you to be part of a winning team than to be out there collecting the glory for yourself.

You are dependable, kind, loving and peerless in your defence of those you take to. All of these are incredible resources when used in the correct way. Perhaps most important of all is your ability to get others on your side. In this you cannot be matched.

Beneath the surface

Everyone instinctively knows that there is something very important going on beneath the surface of the Piscean mind, though working out exactly what it might be is a different kettle of fish altogether. The fact is that you are very secretive about yourself and tend to give very little away. There are occasions when this tendency can be a saving grace, but others where it is definitely a great disadvantage. What isn't hard to see is your natural sympathy and your desire to help those in trouble. There's no end gain here, it's simply the way you are. Your inspiration to do anything is rarely rooted in what your own prize is likely to be. In your soul you are poetical, deeply romantic and inextricably tied to the forces and cycles of the world that brought you to birth.

Despite your capacity for single-minded concentration in some matters, you are often subject to mental confusion. Rational considerations often take second place to intuitive foresight and even inspiration. Making leaps in logic isn't at all unusual for you and forms part of the way you judge the world and deal with it.

If you really want to get on in life, and to gain the most you can from your interactions with others, you need to be very truthful in your approach. Somehow or other that means finding out what is really going on in your mind and explaining it to those around you. This is never going to be an easy process, partly because of your naturally secretive ways. Actually some astrologers overplay the tendency of Pisces to keep its secrets. A great deal of the time you simply don't think you have anything to say that would interest others and you always lack confidence in your own judgements. This is a shame because you rarely proceed without thinking carefully and don't often make glaring mistakes.

Many Pisceans develop an ingrained tendency to believe themselves inadequate in some way. Once again this is something you should fight against. Knowing others better, and allowing them to get to know you, might cause you to feel less quirky or strange. Whether you realise it or not you have a natural magnetism that draws others towards you. Try to spend rather less time thinking – though without losing that Piscean ability to meditate which is central to your well-being. If you allow the fascinating world of the Piscean mind to be shared by the people you come to trust, you should become more understandable to people who really want to like you even more.

Making the best of yourself

It must be remembered that the zodiac sign of Pisces represents two Fishes, tethered by a cord but constantly trying to break away from each other. This says a great deal about the basic Piscean nature. The inward, contemplative side of your personality is often at odds with the more gregarious and chatty qualities you also possess. Learning about this duality of nature can go at least part of the way towards dealing with it.

Although you often exhibit a distinct lack of self-confidence in your dealings with the world at large, you are, at heart, quite adept, flexible and able to cope under almost any circumstance. All that is really required in order to have a positive influence on life and to be successful is for you to realise what you are capable of achieving. Alas this isn't quite as easy as it might appear, because the introspective depths of your nature make you think too much and cause you to avoid the very actions that would get you noticed more. This can be something of a dilemma for Pisces, though it is certainly not insurmountable.

Never be afraid to allow your sensitivity to show. It is one of your greatest assets and it is part of the reason why other people love you so much – far more, in fact, than you probably realise. Your natural warmth, grace and charm are certain to turn heads on those occasions when you can't avoid being watched. The creative qualities that you possess make it possible for you to manufacture harmonious surroundings, both for yourself and for your family, who are very important to you. At the same time you recognise the practical in life and don't mind getting your hands dirty, especially when it comes to helping someone else out of a mess.

One of the best ruses Pisceans can use in order to get over the innate shyness that often attends the sign is to put on an act. Pisceans are very good natural actors and can easily assume the role of another individual. So, in your dealings with the world at large, manufacture a more confident individual, though without leaving out all the wonderful things that make you what you are now. Play this part for all you are worth and you will then truly be making the best of yourself.

The impressions you give

There is absolutely no doubt that you are more popular, admired and even fancied than you could ever believe. Such is the natural modesty of your zodiac sign that you invariably fail to pick up on those little messages coming across from other people that say 'I think you are wonderful'. If we don't believe in ourselves it's difficult for us to accept that others think we are worth their consideration. Failing to realise your worth to the world at large is likely to be your greatest fault and needs to be corrected.

In a way it doesn't matter, when seen from the perspective of others. What they observe is a warm-hearted individual. Your magnetic personality is always on display, whether you intend it to be or not, which is another reason why you tend to attract far more attention than you would sometimes elicit. Most Pisceans are quite sexy, another quality that is bound to come across to the people you meet, at least some of whom would be willing to jump through hoops if you were to command it.

In short, what you show, and what you think you are, could be two entirely different things. If you don't believe this to be the case you need to carry out a straw poll amongst some of the people you know. Ask them to write down all your qualities as they see them. The result will almost certainly surprise you and demonstrate that you are far more capable, and loveable, than you believe yourself to be. Armed with this knowledge you can walk forward in life with more confidence and feel as content inside as you appear to be when viewed by the world at large.

People rely heavily on you. That much at least you will have noticed in a day-to-day sense. They do so because they know how well you deal with almost any situation. Even in a crisis you show your true colours and that's part of the reason why so many Piscean people find themselves involved in the medical profession. You are viewed as being stronger than you believe yourself to be, which is why everyone tends to be so surprised when they discover that you are vulnerable and inclined to worry.

The way forward

You have a great deal to offer the world, even if you don't always appreciate how much. Although you are capable of being shy and introverted on occasions, you are equally likely to be friendly, chatty and very co-operative. You settle to just about any task, though you do possess a sense of freedom that makes it difficult for you to be cooped up in the same place for days and weeks at a stretch. You prefer the sort of tasks that allow your own natural proclivities to shine out, and you exhibit an instinctive creative tendency in almost anything you do.

Use your natural popularity to the full. People are always willing to put themselves out on your behalf, mainly because they know how generous you are and want to repay you for some previous favour. You should never be too proud to accept this sort of proffered help and must avoid running away with the idea that you are unequal to any reasonable task that you set yourself.

It's true that some of your thoughts are extremely deep and that you can get yourself into something of a brown study on occasions, which can be translated by the world around you as depression. However, you are far more stable than you probably believe yourself to be because Pisces is actually one of the toughest of the zodiac signs.

Because you are born of a Water sign it is likely that you would take great delight in living near the sea, or some other large body of water. This isn't essential to your well-being but it does feed your imagination. The vastness of nature in all its forms probably appeals to you in any case and most Pisceans love the natural world with its staggering diversity.

In love you are ardent and sincere, but you do need to make sure that you choose the right individual to suit you. Pisceans often settle for a protecting arm, but if this turns out to be stifling, trouble could follow. You would find it hard to live with anyone who didn't have at least a degree of your sensitivity, and you need a partner who will allow you to retain that sense of inner freedom that is so vital to your well-being.

Make the most of the many gifts and virtues that nature has bestowed upon you and don't be afraid to let people know what you really are. Actually establishing this in the first place isn't easy for you. Pisceans respond well to almost any form of meditation, which is not surprising because the sign of the Fishes is the most spiritually motivated zodiac sign of them all. When you know yourself fully you generate a personality that is an inspiration to everyone.

PISCES ON THE CUSP

Old Moore is often asked how astrological profiles are altered for those people born at either the beginning or the end of a zodiac sign, or, more properly, on the cusps of a sign. In the case of Pisces this would be on the 20th of February and for two or three days after, and similarly at the end of the sign, probably from the 18th to the 20th of March. In this year's Astral Diaries, once again, Old Moore sets out to explain the differences regarding cuspid signs.

The Aquarius Cusp – February 20th to 22nd

This tends to be a generally happy combination of signs, even if some of the people you come into contact with find you rather difficult to understand from time to time. You are quite capable of cutting a dash, as any Aquarian would be, and yet at the same time you have the quiet and contemplative qualities more typified by Pisces. You tend to be seen as an immensely attractive person, even if you are the last one in the world to accept this fact. People find you to be friendly, very approachable and good company in almost any social or personal setting. It isn't hard for you to get on with others, though since you are not so naturally quiet as Pisces when taken alone, you are slightly more willing to speak your mind and to help out, though usually in a very diplomatic manner.

At work you are very capable and many people with this combination find themselves working on behalf of humanity as a whole. Thus work in social services, hospitals or charities really suits the unique combinations thrown up by this sign mixture. Management is right up your street, though there are times when your conception of popularity takes the foremost place in your mind. Occasionally this could take the edge off executive decisions. A careful attention to detail shows you in a position to get things done, even jobs that others shun. You don't really care for getting your hands dirty but will tackle almost any task if you know it to be necessary. Being basically self-sufficient, you also love the company of others, and it is this adaptability that is the hallmark of success to Aquarian-cusp Pisceans.

Few people actually know you as well as they think they do because the waters of your nature run quite deep. Your real task in life is to let the world know how you feel, something you fight shy of doing now and again. There are positive gains in your life, brought about as a result of your adaptable and pleasing nature. Aquarius present in the nature allows Pisces to act at its best.

The Aries Cusp – March 18th to 20th

This is a Piscean with attitude and probably one of the most difficult zodiac sign combinations to be understood, not only by those people with whom you come into contact but clearly by yourself too. If there are any problems thrown up here they come from the fact that Pisces and Aries have such different ways of expressing themselves to the world at large. Aries is very upfront, dynamic and dominant, all factors that are simply diametrically opposed to the way Pisces thinks and behaves. So the real task in life is to find ways to combine the qualities of Pisces and Aries, in a way that suits the needs of both and without becoming totally confused with regard to your basic nature.

The problem is usually solved by a compartmentation of life. For example, many people with this combination will show the Aries qualities strongly at work, whilst dropping into the Piscean mode socially and at home. This may invariably be the case but there are bound to be times when the underlying motivations become mixed, which can confuse those with whom you come into contact.

Having said all of this you can be the least selfish and most successful individual when you are fighting for the rights of others. This is the zodiac combination of the true social reformer, the genuine politician and the committed pacifist. It seems paradoxical to suggest that someone could fight tenaciously for peace, but this is certainly true in your case. You have excellent executive skills and yet retain an ability to tell other people what they should be doing, in fairly strident terms, usually without upsetting anyone. There is a degree of genuine magic about you that makes you very attractive and there is likely to be more than one love affair in your life. A steadfast view of romance may not be naturally present within your basic nature but like so much else you can 'train' this quality into existence.

Personal success is likely, but it probably doesn't matter all that much in a material sense. The important thing to you is being needed by the world at large.

PISCES AND ITS ASCENDANTS

The nature of every individual on the planet is composed of the rich variety of zodiac signs and planetary positions that were present at the time of their birth. Your Sun sign, which in your case is Pisces, is one of the many factors when it comes to assessing the unique person you are. Probably the most important consideration, other than your Sun sign, is to establish the zodiac sign that was rising over the eastern horizon at the time that you were born. This is your Ascending or Rising sign. Most popular astrology fails to take account of the Ascendant, and yet its importance remains with you from the very moment of your birth, through every day of your life. The Ascendant is evident in the way you approach the world, and so, when meeting a person for the first time, it is this astrological influence that you are most likely to notice first. Our Ascending sign essentially represents what we appear to be, while the Sun sign is what we feel inside ourselves.

The Ascendant also has the potential for modifying our overall nature. For example, if you were born at a time of day when Pisces was passing over the eastern horizon (this would be around the time of dawn) then you would be classed as a double Pisces. As such, you would typify this zodiac sign, both internally and in your dealings with others. However, if your Ascendant sign turned out to be a Fire sign, such as Aries, there would be a profound alteration of nature, away from the expected qualities of Pisces.

One of the reasons why popular astrology often ignores the Ascendant is that it has always been rather difficult to establish. Old Moore has found a way to make this possible by devising an easy-to-use table, which you will find on page 158 of this book. Using this, you can establish your Ascendant sign at a glance. You will need to know your rough time of birth, then it is simply a case of following the instructions.

For those readers who have no idea of their time of birth it might be worth allowing a good friend, or perhaps your partner, to read through the section that follows this introduction. Someone who deals with you on a regular basis may easily discover your Ascending sign, even though you could have some difficulty establishing it for yourself. A good understanding of this component of your nature is essential if you want to be aware of that 'other person' who is responsible for the way you make contact with the world at large. Your Sun sign, Ascendant sign, and the other pointers in this book will, together, allow you a far better understanding of what makes you tick as an individual. Peeling back the different layers of your astrological make-up can be an enlightening experience, and the Ascendant may represent one of the most important layers of all.

Pisces with Pisces Ascendant

You are a kind and considerate person who would do almost anything to please the people around you. Creative and extremely perceptive, nobody knows the twists and turns of human nature better than you do, and you make it your business to serve humanity in any way you can. Not everyone understands what makes you tick, and part of the reason for this state of affairs is that you are often not really quite 'in' the world as much as the people you encounter in a day-to-day sense. At work you are generally cheerful, though you can be very quiet on occasions, but since you are consistent in this regard, you don't attract adverse attention or accusations of being moody, as some other variants of Pisces sometimes do. Confusion can beset you on occasions, especially when you are trying to reconcile your own opposing needs. There are certain moments of discontent to be encountered which so often come from trying to please others, even when to do so goes against your own instincts.

As age and experience add to your personal armoury you relax more with the world and find yourself constantly sought out for words of wisdom. The vast majority of people care for you deeply.

Pisces with Aries Ascendant

Although not an easy combination to deal with, the Pisces with an Aries Ascendant does bring something very special to the world in the way of natural understanding allied to practical assistance. It's true that you can sometimes be a dreamer, but there is nothing wrong with that as long as you have the ability to turn some of your wishes into reality, and this you are usually able to do, often for the sake of those around you. Conversation comes easily to you, though you also possess a slightly wistful and poetic side to your nature, which is attractive to the many people who call you a friend. A natural entertainer, you bring a sense of the comic to the often serious qualities of Aries, though without losing the determination that typifies the sign.

In relationships you are ardent, sincere and supportive, with a social conscience that sometimes finds you fighting the battles of the less privileged members of society. Family is important to you and this is a combination that invariably leads to parenthood. Away from the cut and thrust of everyday life you relax more fully, and think about matters more deeply than more typical Aries types might.

Pisces with Taurus Ascendant

You are clearly a very sensitive type of person and that sometimes makes it rather difficult for others to know how they might best approach you. Private and deep, you are nevertheless socially inclined on many occasions. However, because your nature is bottomless it is possible that some types would actually accuse you of being shallow. How can this come about? Well, it's simple really. The fact is that you rarely show anyone what is going on in the deepest recesses of your mind and so your responses can appear to be trite or even ill-considered. This is far from the truth, as those who are allowed into the 'inner sanctum' would readily admit. You are something of a sensualist, and relish staying in bed late and simply pleasing yourself for days on end. However, you have Taurean traits so you desire a tidy environment in which to live your usually long life.

You are able to deal with the routine aspects of life quite well and can be a capable worker once you are up and firing on all cylinders. It is very important that you maintain an interest in what you are doing, because the recesses of your dreamy mind can sometimes appear to be infinitely more attractive. Your imagination is second to none and this fact can often be turned to your advantage.

Pisces with Gemini Ascendant

There is great duality inherent in this combination, and sometimes this can cause a few problems. Part of the trouble stems from the fact that you often fail to realise what you want from life, and you could also be accused of failing to take the time out to think things through carefully enough. You are reactive, and although you have every bit of the natural charm that typifies the sign of Gemini, you are more prone to periods of self-doubt and confusion. However, you should not allow these facts to get you down too much, because you are also genuinely loved and have a tremendous capacity to look after others, a factor which is more important to you than any other. It's true that personal relationships can sometimes be a cause of difficulty for you, partly because your constant need to know what makes other people tick could drive them up the wall. Accepting people at face value seems to be the best key to happiness of a personal sort, and there are occasions when your very real and natural intuition has to be put on hold.

It's likely that you are an original, particularly in the way you dress. An early rebellious stage often gives way to a more comfortable form of eccentricity. When you are at your best, just about everyone adores you.

Pisces with Cancer Ascendant

A deep, double Water-sign combination this, and it might serve to make you a very misunderstood, though undoubtedly popular, individual. You are anxious to make a good impression, probably too keen under certain circumstances, and you do everything you can to help others, even if you don't know them very well. It's true that you are deeply sensitive and quite easily brought to tears by the suffering of this most imperfect world that we inhabit. Fatigue can be a problem, though this is somewhat nullified by the fact that you can withdraw completely into the deep recesses of your own mind when it becomes necessary to do so.

You may not be the most gregarious person in the world, simply because it isn't easy for you to put some of your most important considerations into words. This is easier when you are in the company of people you know and trust, though even trust is a commodity that is difficult for you to find, particularly since you may have been hurt by being too willing to share your thoughts early in life. With age comes wisdom and maturity, and the older you are, the better you will learn to handle this potent and demanding combination. You will never go short of either friends or would-be lovers, and may be one of the most magnetic types of both Cancer and Pisces.

Pisces with Leo Ascendant

You are a very sensitive soul, on occasions too much so for your own good. However, there is not a better advocate for the rights of humanity than you represent and you constantly do what you can to support the downtrodden and oppressed. Good causes are your thing and there are likely to be many in your life. You will probably find yourself pushed to the front of almost any enterprise of which you are a part because, despite the deeper qualities of Pisces, you are a natural leader. Even on those occasions when it feels as though you lack confidence, you manage to muddle through somehow and your smile is as broad as the day. Few sign combinations are more loved than this one, mainly because you do not have a malicious bone in your body, and will readily forgive and forget, which the Lion on its own often will not.

Although you are capable of acting on impulse, you do so from a deep sense of moral conviction, so that most of your endeavours are designed to suit other people too. They recognise this fact and will push much support back in your direction. Even when you come across troubles in your life you manage to find ways to sort them out, and will invariably notice something new to smile about on the way. Your sensitivity rating is massive and you can easily be moved to tears.

Pisces with Virgo Ascendant

You might have been accused on occasions of being too sensitive for your own good, a charge that is not entirely without foundation. Certainly you are very understanding of the needs of others, sometimes to the extent that you put everything aside to help them. This would also be true in the case of charities, for you care very much about the world and the people who cling tenaciously to its surface. Your ability to love on a one-to-one basis knows no bounds, though you may not discriminate as much as you could, particularly when young, and might have one or two false starts in the love stakes. You don't always choose to verbalise your thoughts and this can cause problems, because there is always so much going on in your mind and Virgo especially needs good powers of communication. Pisces is quieter and you need to force yourself to say what you think when the explanation is important.

You would never betray a confidence and sometimes take on rather more for the sake of your friends than is strictly good for you. This is not a fault but can cause you problems all the same. Because you are so intuitive there is little that escapes your attention, though you should avoid being pessimistic about your insights. Changes of scenery suit you and travel would bring out the best in what can be a repressed nature.

Pisces with Libra Ascendant

An Air and Water combination, you are not easy to understand and have depths that show at times, surprising those people who thought they already knew what you were. You will always keep people guessing and are just as likely to hitchhike around Europe as you are to hold down a steady job, both of which you would undertake with the same degree of commitment and success. Usually young at heart, but always carrying the potential for an old head on young shoulders, you are something of a paradox and not at all easy for totally 'straight' types to understand. But you always make an impression, and tend to be very attractive to members of the opposite sex.

In matters of health you do have to be a little careful because you dissipate much nervous energy and can sometimes be inclined to push yourself too hard, at least in a mental sense. Frequent periods of rest and meditation will do you the world of good and should improve your level of wisdom, which tends to be fairly high already. Much of your effort in life is expounded on behalf of humanity as a whole, for you care deeply, love totally and always give of your best. Whatever your faults and failings might be, you are one of the most popular people around.

Pisces with Scorpio Ascendant

You stand a chance of disappearing so deep into yourself that other people would need one of those long ladders that cave explorers use to even find you. It isn't really your fault, because both Scorpio and Pisces, as Water signs, are difficult to understand and you have them both. But that doesn't mean that you should be content to remain in the dark, and the warmth of your nature is all you need to shine a light on the wonderful qualities you possess. But the primary word of warning is that you must put yourself on display and allow others to know what you are, before their appreciation of these facts becomes apparent.

As a server of the world you are second to none and it is hard to find a person with this combination who is not, in some way, looking out for the people around them. Immensely attractive to others, you are also one of the most sought-after lovers. Much of this has to do with your deep and abiding charm, but the air of mystery that surrounds you also helps. Some of you will marry too early, and end up regretting the fact, though the majority of people with Scorpio and Pisces will find the love they deserve in the end. You are able, just, firm but fair, though a sucker for a hard luck story and as kind as the day is long. It's hard to imagine how so many good points could be ignored by others.

Pisces with Sagittarius Ascendant

A very attractive combination this, because the more dominant qualities of the Archer are somehow mellowed-out by the caring Water-sign qualities of the Fishes. You can be very outgoing, but there is always a deeper side to your nature that allows others to know that you are thinking about them. Few people could fall out with either your basic nature or your attitude to the world at large, even though there are depths to your nature that may not be easily understood. You are capable, have a good executive ability and can work hard to achieve your objectives, even if you get a little disillusioned on the way. Much of your life is given over to helping those around you and there is a great tendency for you to work for and on behalf of humanity as a whole. A sense of community is brought to most of what you do and you enjoy co-operation. Although you have the natural ability to attract people to you, the Pisces half of your nature makes you just a little more reserved in personal matters than might otherwise be the case. More careful in your choices than either sign taken alone, you still have to make certain that your motivations when commencing a personal relationship are the right ones. You love to be happy, and to offer gifts of happiness to others.

Pisces with Capricorn Ascendant

You are certainly not the easiest person in the world to understand, mainly because your nature is so deep and your personality so complicated, that others are somewhat intimidated at the prospect of staring into this abyss. All the same your friendly nature is attractive, and there will always be people around who are fascinated by the sheer magnetic quality that is intrinsic to this zodiac mix. Sentimental and extremely kind, there is no limit to the extent of your efforts on behalf of a deserving world, though there are some people around who wonder at your commitment and who may ridicule you a little for your staying-power, even in the face of some adversity. At work you are very capable, will work long and hard, and can definitely expect a greater degree of financial and practical success than Pisces when taken alone. Routines don't bother you too much, though you do need regular periods of introspection, which help to recharge low batteries and a battered self-esteem. In affairs of the heart you are given to impulse, which belies the more careful qualities of Capricorn. However, the determination remains intact and you are quite capable of chasing rainbows round and round the same field, never realising that you can't get to the end of them. Generally speaking you are an immensely lovable person and a great favourite to many.

Pisces with Aquarius Ascendant

Here we find the originality of Aquarius balanced by the very sensitive qualities of Pisces, and it makes for a very interesting combination. When it comes to understanding other people you are second to none, but it's certain that you are more instinctive than either Pisces or Aquarius when taken alone. You are better at routines than Aquarius, but also relish a challenge more than the typical Piscean would. Active and enterprising, you tend to know what you want from life, but consideration of others, and the world at large, will always be part of the scenario. People with this combination often work on behalf of humanity and are to be found in social work, the medical profession and religious institutions. As far as beliefs are concerned you don't conform to established patterns, and yet may get closer to the truth of the Creator than many deep theological thinkers have ever been able to do. Acting on impulse as much as you do means that not everyone understands the way your mind works, but your popularity will invariably see you through.

Passionate and deeply sensitive, you are able to negotiate the twists and turns of a romantic life that is hardly likely to be run-of-the-mill. In the end, however, you should certainly be able to find a very deep personal and spiritual happiness.

THE MOON AND THE PART IT PLAYS IN YOUR LIFE

In astrology the Moon is probably the single most important heavenly body after the Sun. Its unique position, as partner to the Earth on its journey around the solar system, means that the Moon appears to pass through the signs of the zodiac extremely quickly. The zodiac position of the Moon at the time of your birth plays a great part in personal character and is especially significant in the build-up of your emotional nature.

Sun Moon Cycles

The first lunar cycle deals with the part the position of the Moon plays relative to your Sun sign. I have made the fluctuations of this pattern easy for you to understand by means of a simple cyclic graph. It appears on the first page of each 'Your Month At A Glance', under the title 'Highs and Lows'. The graph displays the lunar cycle and you will soon learn to understand how its movements have a bearing on your level of energy and your abilities.

Your Own Moon Sign

Discovering the position of the Moon at the time of your birth has always been notoriously difficult because tracking the complex zodiac positions of the Moon is not easy. This process has been reduced to three simple stages with Old Moore's unique Lunar Tables. A breakdown of the Moon's zodiac positions can be found from page 25 onwards, so that once you know what your Moon Sign is, you can see what part this plays in the overall build-up of your personal character.

If you follow the instructions on the next page you will soon be able to work out exactly what zodiac sign the Moon occupied on the day that you were born and you can then go on to compare the reading for this position with those of your Sun sign and your Ascendant. It is partly the comparison between these three important positions that goes towards making you the unique individual you are.

HOW TO DISCOVER YOUR MOON SIGN

This is a three-stage process. You may need a pen and a piece of paper but if you follow the instructions below the process should only take a minute or so.

STAGE 1 First of all you need to know the Moon Age at the time of your birth. If you look at Moon Table 1, on page 23, you will find all the years between 1911 and 2009 down the left side. Find the year of your birth and then trace across to the right to the month of your birth. Where the two intersect you will find a number. This is the date of the New Moon in the month that you were born. You now need to count forward the number of days between the New Moon and your own birthday. For example, if the New Moon in the month of your birth was shown as being the 6th and you were born on the 20th, your Moon Age Day would be 14. If the New Moon in the month of your birth came after your birthday, you need to count forward from the New Moon in the previous month. If you were born in a Leap Year, remember to count the 29th February. You can tell if your birth year was a Leap Year if the last two digits can be divided by four. Whatever the result, jot this number down so that you do not forget it.

STAGE 2 Take a look at Moon Table 2 on page 24. Down the left hand column look for the date of your birth. Now trace across to the month of your birth. Where the two meet you will find a letter. Copy this letter down alongside your Moon Age Day.

STAGE 3 Moon Table 3 on page 24 will supply you with the zodiac sign the Moon occupied on the day of your birth. Look for your Moon Age Day down the left hand column and then for the letter you found in Stage 2. Where the two converge you will find a zodiac sign and this is the sign occupied by the Moon on the day that you were born.

Your Zodiac Moon Sign Explained

You will find a profile of all zodiac Moon Signs on pages 25 to 28, showing in yet another way how astrology helps to make you into the individual that you are. In each daily entry of the Astral Diary you can find the zodiac position of the Moon for every day of the year. This also allows you to discover your lunar birthdays. Since the Moon passes through all the signs of the zodiac in about a month, you can expect something like twelve lunar birthdays each year. At these times you are likely to be emotionally steady and able to make the sort of decisions that have real, lasting value.

MOON TABLE 1

YEAR	JAN	FEB	MAR	YEAR	JAN	FEB	MAR	YEAR	JAN	FEB	MAR
1911	29	28	30	1944	25	24	24	1977	19	18	19
1912	18	17	19	1945	14	12	14	1978	9	7	9
1913	7	6	7	1946	3	2	3	1979	27	26	27
1914	25	24	26	1947	21	19	21	1980	16	15	16
1915	15	15	14	1948	11	9	11	1981	6	4	6
1916	5	3	5	1949	29	27	29	1982	25	23	24
1917	24	22	23	1950	18	16	18	1983	14	13	14
1918	12	11	12	1951	7	6	7	1984	3	1	2
1919	1/31	–	2/31	1952	26	25	25	1985	21	19	21
1920	21	19	20	1953	15	14	15	1986	10	9	10
1921	9	8	9	1954	5	3	5	1987	29	28	29
1922	27	26	28	1955	24	22	24	1988	18	17	18
1923	17	15	17	1956	13	11	12	1989	7	6	7
1924	6	5	5	1957	1/30	–	1/31	1990	26	25	26
1925	24	23	24	1958	19	18	20	1991	15	14	15
1926	14	12	14	1959	9	7	9	1992	4	3	4
1927	3	2	3	1960	27	26	27	1993	24	22	24
1928	21	19	21	1961	16	15	16	1994	11	10	12
1929	11	9	11	1962	6	5	6	1995	1/31	–	1/30
1930	29	28	30	1963	25	23	25	1996	19	18	19
1931	18	17	19	1964	14	13	14	1997	9	7	9
1932	7	6	7	1965	3	1	2	1998	27	26	27
1933	25	24	26	1966	21	19	21	1999	16	15	16
1934	15	14	15	1967	10	9	10	2000	6	4	6
1935	5	3	5	1968	29	28	29	2001	24	23	25
1936	24	22	23	1969	19	17	18	2002	13	12	13
1937	12	11	12	1970	7	6	7	2003	3	1	2
1938	1/31	–	2/31	1971	26	25	26	2004	21	20	21
1939	20	19	20	1972	15	14	15	2005	10	9	10
1940	9	8	9	1973	5	4	5	2006	29	28	29
1941	27	26	27	1974	24	22	24	2007	18	16	18
1942	16	15	16	1975	12	11	12	2008	8	6	7
1943	6	4	6	1976	1/31	29	30	2009	26	25	26

TABLE 2

DAY	FEB	MAR
1	D	F
2	D	G
3	D	G
4	D	G
5	D	G
6	D	G
7	D	G
8	D	G
9	D	G
10	E	G
11	E	G
12	E	H
13	E	H
14	E	H
15	E	H
16	E	H
17	E	H
18	E	H
19	E	H
20	F	H
21	F	H
22	F	I
23	F	I
24	F	I
25	F	I
26	F	I
27	F	I
28	F	I
29	F	I
30	–	I
31	–	I

MOON TABLE 3

M/D	D	E	F	G	H	I	J
0	AQ	PI	PI	PI	AR	AR	AR
1	PI	PI	PI	AR	AR	AR	TA
2	PI	PI	AR	AR	AR	TA	TA
3	PI	AR	AR	AR	TA	TA	TA
4	AR	AR	AR	TA	TA	GE	GE
5	AR	TA	TA	TA	GE	GE	GE
6	TA	TA	TA	GE	GE	GE	CA
7	TA	TA	GE	GE	GE	CA	CA
8	TA	GE	GE	GE	CA	CA	CA
9	GE	GE	CA	CA	CA	CA	LE
10	GE	CA	CA	CA	LE	LE	LE
11	CA	CA	CA	LE	LE	LE	VI
12	CA	CA	LE	LE	LE	VI	VI
13	LE	LE	LE	LE	VI	VI	VI
14	LE	LE	VI	VI	VI	LI	LI
15	LE	VI	VI	VI	LI	LI	LI
16	VI	VI	VI	LI	LI	LI	SC
17	VI	VI	LI	LI	LI	SC	SC
18	VI	LI	LI	LI	SC	SC	SC
19	LI	LI	LI	SC	SC	SC	SA
20	LI	SC	SC	SC	SA	SA	SA
21	SC	SC	SC	SA	SA	SA	CP
22	SC	SC	SA	SA	SA	CP	CP
23	SC	SA	SA	SA	CP	CP	CP
24	SA	SA	SA	CP	CP	CP	AQ
25	SA	CP	CP	CP	AQ	AQ	AQ
26	CP	CP	CP	AQ	AQ	AQ	PI
27	CP	AQ	AQ	AQ	AQ	PI	PI
28	AQ	AQ	AQ	AQ	PI	PI	PI
29	AQ	AQ	AQ	PI	PI	PI	AR

AR = Aries, TA = Taurus, GE = Gemini, CA = Cancer, LE = Leo, VI = Virgo, LI = Libra, SC = Scorpio, SA = Sagittarius, CP = Capricorn, AQ = Aquarius, PI = Pisces

MOON SIGNS

Moon in Aries

You have a strong imagination, courage, determination and a desire to do things in your own way and forge your own path through life.

Originality is a key attribute; you are seldom stuck for ideas although your mind is changeable and you could take the time to focus on individual tasks. Often quick-tempered, you take orders from few people and live life at a fast pace. Avoid health problems by taking regular time out for rest and relaxation.

Emotionally, it is important that you talk to those you are closest to and work out your true feelings. Once you discover that people are there to help, there is less necessity for you to do everything yourself.

Moon in Taurus

The Moon in Taurus gives you a courteous and friendly manner, which means you are likely to have many friends.

The good things in life mean a lot to you, as Taurus is an Earth sign that delights in experiences which please the senses. Hence you are probably a lover of good food and drink, which may in turn mean you need to keep an eye on the bathroom scales, especially as looking good is also important to you.

Emotionally you are fairly stable and you stick by your own standards. Taureans do not respond well to change. Intuition also plays an important part in your life.

Moon in Gemini

You have a warm-hearted character, sympathetic and eager to help others. At times reserved, you can also be articulate and chatty: this is part of the paradox of Gemini, which always brings duplicity to the nature. You are interested in current affairs, have a good intellect, and are good company and likely to have many friends. Most of your friends have a high opinion of you and would be ready to defend you should the need arise. However, this is usually unnecessary, as you are quite capable of defending yourself in any verbal confrontation.

Travel is important to your inquisitive mind and you find intellectual stimulus in mixing with people from different cultures. You also gain much from reading, writing and the arts but you do need plenty of rest and relaxation in order to avoid fatigue.

Moon in Cancer

The Moon in Cancer at the time of birth is a fortunate position as Cancer is the Moon's natural home. This means that the qualities of compassion and understanding given by the Moon are especially enhanced in your nature, and you are friendly and sociable and cope well with emotional pressures. You cherish home and family life, and happily do the domestic tasks. Your surroundings are important to you and you hate squalor and filth. You are likely to have a love of music and poetry.

Your basic character, although at times changeable like the Moon itself, depends on symmetry. You aim to make your surroundings comfortable and harmonious, for yourself and those close to you.

Moon in Leo

The best qualities of the Moon and Leo come together to make you warm-hearted, fair, ambitious and self-confident. With good organisational abilities, you invariably rise to a position of responsibility in your chosen career. This is fortunate as you don't enjoy being an 'also-ran' and would rather be an important part of a small organisation than a menial in a large one.

You should be lucky in love, and happy, provided you put in the effort to make a comfortable home for yourself and those close to you. It is likely that you will have a love of pleasure, sport, music and literature. Life brings you many rewards, most of them as a direct result of your own efforts, although you may be luckier than average and ready to make the best of any situation.

Moon in Virgo

You are endowed with good mental abilities and a keen receptive memory, but you are never ostentatious or pretentious. Naturally quite reserved, you still have many friends, especially of the opposite sex. Marital relationships must be discussed carefully and worked at so that they remain harmonious, as personal attachments can be a problem if you do not give them your full attention.

Talented and persevering, you possess artistic qualities and are a good homemaker. Earning your honours through genuine merit, you work long and hard towards your objectives but show little pride in your achievements. Many short journeys will be undertaken in your life.

Moon in Libra

With the Moon in Libra you are naturally popular and make friends easily. People like you, probably more than you realise, you bring fun to a party and are a natural diplomat. For all its good points, Libra is not the most stable of astrological signs and, as a result, your emotions can be a little unstable too. Therefore, although the Moon in Libra is said to be good for love and marriage, your Sun sign and Rising sign will have an important effect on your emotional and loving qualities.

You must remember to relate to others in your decision-making. Co-operation is crucial because Libra represents the 'balance' of life that can only be achieved through harmonious relationships. Conformity is not easy for you because Libra, an Air sign, likes its independence.

Moon in Scorpio

Some people might call you pushy. In fact, all you really want to do is to live life to the full and protect yourself and your family from the pressures of life. Take care to avoid giving the impression of being sarcastic or impulsive and use your energies wisely and constructively.

You have great courage and you invariably achieve your goals by force of personality and sheer effort. You are fond of mystery and are good at predicting the outcome of situations and events. Travel experiences can be beneficial to you.

You may experience problems if you do not take time to examine your motives in a relationship, and also if you allow jealousy, always a feature of Scorpio, to cloud your judgement.

Moon in Sagittarius

The Moon in Sagittarius helps to make you a generous individual with humanitarian qualities and a kind heart. Restlessness may be intrinsic as your mind is seldom still. Perhaps because of this, you have a need for change that could lead you to several major moves during your adult life. You are not afraid to stand your ground when you know your judgement is right, you speak directly and have good intuition.

At work you are quick, efficient and versatile and so you make an ideal employee. You need work to be intellectually demanding and do not enjoy tedious routines.

In relationships, you anger quickly if faced with stupidity or deception, though you are just as quick to forgive and forget. Emotionally, there are times when your heart rules your head.

Moon in Capricorn

The Moon in Capricorn makes you popular and likely to come into the public eye in some way. The watery Moon is not entirely comfortable in the Earth sign of Capricorn and this may lead to some difficulties in the early years of life. An initial lack of creative ability and indecision must be overcome before the true qualities of patience and perseverance inherent in Capricorn can show through.

You have good administrative ability and are a capable worker, and if you are careful you can accumulate wealth. But you must be cautious and take professional advice in partnerships, as you are open to deception. You may be interested in social or welfare work, which suit your organisational skills and sympathy for others.

Moon in Aquarius

The Moon in Aquarius makes you an active and agreeable person with a friendly, easy-going nature. Sympathetic to the needs of others, you flourish in a laid-back atmosphere. You are broad-minded, fair and open to suggestion, although sometimes you have an unconventional quality which others can find hard to understand.

You are interested in the strange and curious, and in old articles and places. You enjoy trips to these places and gain much from them. Political, scientific and educational work interests you and you might choose a career in science or technology.

Money-wise, you make gains through innovation and concentration and Lunar Aquarians often tackle more than one job at a time. In love you are kind and honest.

Moon in Pisces

You have a kind, sympathetic nature, somewhat retiring at times, but you always take account of others' feelings and help when you can.

Personal relationships may be problematic, but as life goes on you can learn from your experiences and develop a better understanding of yourself and the world around you.

You have a fondness for travel, appreciate beauty and harmony and hate disorder and strife. You may be fond of literature and would make a good writer or speaker yourself. You have a creative imagination and may come across as an incurable romantic. You have strong intuition, maybe bordering on a mediumistic quality, which sets you apart from the mass. You may not be rich in cash terms, but your personal gifts are worth more than gold.

PISCES IN LOVE

Discover how compatible in love you are with people from the same and other signs of the zodiac. Five stars equals a match made in heaven!

Pisces meets Pisces

Pisceans are easy-going and get on well with most people, so when two Pisceans get together, harmony is invariably the result. While this isn't the most dynamic relationship, there is mutual understanding, and a desire to please on both sides. Neither partner is likely to be overbearing or selfish. Family responsibilities should be happily shared and home surroundings will be comfortable, but never pretentious. One of the better pairings for the sign of the Fishes. Star rating: *****

Pisces meets Aries

Still waters run deep, and they don't come much deeper than Pisces. Although these signs share the same quadrant of the zodiac, they have little in common. Pisces is a dreamer, a romantic idealist with steady and spiritual goals. Aries needs to be on the move, and has very different ideals. It's hard to see how a relationship could develop but, with patience, there is a chance that things might work out. Pisces needs incentive, and Aries may be the sign to offer it. Star rating: **

Pisces meets Taurus

No problem here, unless both parties come from the quieter side of their respective signs. Most of the time Taurus and Pisces would live comfortably together, offering mutual support and deep regard. Taurus can offer the personal qualities that Pisces craves, whilst Pisces understands and copes with the Bull's slightly stubborn qualities. Taurus is likely to travel in Piscean company, so there is a potential for wide-ranging experiences and variety which is essential. There will be some misunderstandings, mainly because Pisces is so deep, but that won't prevent their enduring happiness. Star rating: ***

Pisces meets Gemini

Gemini likes to think of itself as intuitive and intellectual, but it will never understand Pisces' dark depths. Another stumbling block is that both Gemini and Pisces are 'split' signs – the Twins and the two Fishes – which means that both are capable of dual personalities. There won't be any shortage of affection, but the real question has to be how much these people feel they have in common. Pisces is extremely kind, and so is Gemini most of the time. But Pisces does too much soul-searching for Gemini, who might eventually become bored. Star rating: ***

Pisces meets Cancer

This is likely to be a very successful match. Cancer and Pisces are both Water signs, both deep, sensitive and very caring. Pisces loves deeply, and Cancer wants to be loved. There will be few fireworks here, and a very quiet house. But that doesn't mean that either love or action is lacking – the latter of which is just behind closed doors. Family and children are important to both signs and both are prepared to work hard, but Pisces is the more restless of the two and needs the support and security that Cancer offers. Star rating: *****

Pisces meets Leo

Pisces always needs to understand others, which makes Leo feel warm and loved, while Leo sees, to its delight, that Pisces needs to be protected and taken care of. Pisceans are often lacking in self-confidence which is something Leo has to spare, and happily it is often infectious. Pisces' inevitable cares are swept away on a tide of Leonine cheerfulness. This couple's home would be cheerful and full of love, which is beneficial to all family members. This is not a meeting of minds, but rather an understanding and appreciation of differences. Star rating: ****

Pisces meets Virgo

This looks an unpromising match from beginning to end. There are exceptions to every rule, particularly where Pisces is concerned, but these two signs are both so deep it's hard to imagine that they could ever find what makes the other tick. The depth is different in each case: Virgo's ruminations are extremely materialistic, while Pisces exists in a world of deep-felt, poorly expressed emotion. Pisces and Virgo might find they don't talk much, so only in a contemplative, almost monastic, match would they ever get on. Still, in a vast zodiac, anything is possible. Star rating: **

Pisces meets Libra

Libra and Pisces can be extremely fond of each other, even deeply in love, but this alone isn't a stable foundation for long-term success. Pisces is extremely deep and doesn't even know itself very well. Libra may initially find this intriguing but will eventually feel frustrated at being unable to understand the Piscean's emotional and personal feelings. Pisces can be jealous and may find Libra's flightiness difficult, which Libra can't stand. They are great friends and they may make it to the romantic stakes, but when they get there a great deal of effort will be necessary. Star rating: ***

Pisces meets Scorpio

If ever there were two zodiac signs that have a total rapport, it has to be Scorpio and Pisces. They share very similar needs: they are not gregarious and are happy with a little silence, good music and time to contemplate the finer things in life, and both are attracted to family life. Apart, they can have a tendency to wander in a romantic sense, but this is reduced when they come together. They are deep, firm friends who enjoy each other's company and this must lead to an excellent chance of success. These people are surely made for each other! Star rating: *****

Pisces meets Sagittarius

Probably the least likely success story for either sign, which is why it scores so low on the star rating. The basic problem is an almost total lack of understanding. A successful relationship needs empathy and progress towards a shared goal but, although both are eager to please, Pisces is too deep and Sagittarius too flighty – they just don't belong on the same planet! As pals, they have more in common and so a friendship is the best hope of success and happiness. Star rating: *

Pisces meets Capricorn

There is some chance of a happy relationship here, but it will need work on both sides. Capricorn is a go-getter, but likes to plan long term. Pisces is naturally more immediate, but has enough intuition to understand the Goat's thinking. Both have patience, but it will usually be Pisces who chooses to play second fiddle. The quiet nature of both signs might be a problem, as someone will have to take the lead, especially in social situations. Both signs should recognise this fact and accommodate it. Star rating: ***

Pisces meets Aquarius

Zodiac signs that follow each other often have something in common, but this is often not the case with Aquarius and Pisces. Both signs are deeply caring, but in different ways. Pisces is one of the deepest zodiac signs, and Aquarius simply isn't prepared to embark on the journey. Pisceans, meanwhile, would probably find Aquarians superficial and even flippant. On the positive side, there is potential for a well-balanced relationship, but unless one party is untypical of their zodiac sign, it often doesn't get started. Star rating: **

VENUS:
THE PLANET OF LOVE

If you look up at the sky around sunset or sunrise you will often see Venus in close attendance to the Sun. It is arguably one of the most beautiful sights of all and there is little wonder that historically it became associated with the goddess of love. But although Venus does play an important part in the way you view love and in the way others see you romantically, this is only one of the spheres of influence that it enjoys in your overall character.

Venus has a part to play in the more cultured side of your life and has much to do with your appreciation of art, literature, music and general creativity. Even the way you look is responsive to the part of the zodiac that Venus occupied at the start of your life, though this fact is also down to your Sun sign and Ascending sign. If, at the time you were born, Venus occupied one of the more gregarious zodiac signs, you will be more likely to wear your heart on your sleeve, as well as to be more attracted to entertainment, social gatherings and good company. If on the other hand Venus occupied a quiet zodiac sign at the time of your birth, you would tend to be more retiring and less willing to shine in public situations.

It's good to know what part the planet Venus plays in your life for it can have a great bearing on the way you appear to the rest of the world and since we all have to mix with others, you can learn to make the very best of what Venus has to offer you.

One of the great complications in the past has always been trying to establish exactly what zodiac position Venus enjoyed when you were born because the planet is notoriously difficult to track. However, I have solved that problem by creating a table that is exclusive to your Sun sign, which you will find on the following page.

Establishing your Venus sign could not be easier. Just look up the year of your birth on the page opposite and you will see a sign of the zodiac. This was the sign that Venus occupied in the period covered by your sign in that year. If Venus occupied more than one sign during the period, this is indicated by the date on which the sign changed, and the name of the new sign. For instance, if you were born in 1940, Venus was in Aries until the 9th March, after which time it was in Taurus. If you were born before 9th March your Venus sign is Aries, if you were born on or after 9th March, your Venus sign is Taurus. Once you have established the position of Venus at the time of your birth, you can then look in the pages which follow to see how this has a bearing on your life as a whole.

1911 PISCES / 27.2 ARIES
1912 CAPRICORN /
  24.2 AQUARIUS / 19.3 PISCES
1913 ARIES / 7.3 TAURUS
1914 PISCES / 15.3 ARIES
1915 CAPRICORN
1916 ARIES / 10.3 TAURUS
1917 AQUARIUS / 5.3 PISCES
1918 AQUARIUS
1919 PISCES / 27.2 ARIES
1920 CAPRICORN /
  24.2 AQUARIUS / 19.3 PISCES
1921 ARIES / 8.3 TAURUS
1922 PISCES / 14.3 ARIES
1923 CAPRICORN
1924 ARIES / 10.3 TAURUS
1925 AQUARIUS / 4.3 PISCES
1926 AQUARIUS
1927 PISCES / 26.2 ARIES
1928 CAPRICORN /
  23.2 AQUARIUS / 18.3 PISCES
1929 ARIES / 9.3 TAURUS
1930 PISCES / 13.3 ARIES
1931 CAPRICORN
1932 ARIES / 9.3 TAURUS
1933 AQUARIUS / 4.3 PISCES
1934 AQUARIUS
1935 PISCES / 25.2 ARIES
1936 CAPRICORN /
  23.2 AQUARIUS / 18.3 PISCES
1937 ARIES / 10.3 TAURUS
1938 PISCES / 12.3 ARIES
1939 CAPRICORN
1940 ARIES / 9.3 TAURUS
1941 AQUARIUS / 3.3 PISCES
1942 AQUARIUS
1943 PISCES / 25.2 ARIES
1944 CAPRICORN /
  22.2 AQUARIUS / 18.3 PISCES
1945 ARIES / 11.3 TAURUS
1946 PISCES / 11.3 ARIES
1947 CAPRICORN
1948 ARIES / 8.3 TAURUS
1949 AQUARIUS / 3.3 PISCES
1950 AQUARIUS
1951 PISCES / 24.2 ARIES
1952 CAPRICORN /
  22.2 AQUARIUS / 17.3 PISCES
1953 ARIES
1954 PISCES / 11.3 ARIES
1955 CAPRICORN
1956 ARIES / 8.3 TAURUS
1957 AQUARIUS / 2.3 PISCES
1958 CAPRICORN /
  25.2 AQUARIUS
1959 PISCES / 24.2 ARIES
1960 CAPRICORN /
  21.2 AQUARIUS / 17.3 PISCES
1961 ARIES
1962 PISCES / 10.3 ARIES

1963 CAPRICORN
1964 ARIES / 8.3 TAURUS
1965 AQUARIUS / 1.3 PISCES
1966 AQUARIUS
1967 PISCES / 23.2 ARIES
1968 SAGITTARIUS /
  26.1 CAPRICORN
1969 ARIES
1970 PISCES / 10.3 ARIES
1971 CAPRICORN
1972 ARIES / 7.3 TAURUS
1973 AQUARIUS / 1.3 PISCES
1974 CAPRICORN / 2.3 AQUARIUS
1975 PISCES / 23.2 ARIES
1976 SAGITTARIUS /
  26.1 CAPRICORN
1977 ARIES
1978 PISCES / 9.3 ARIES
1979 CAPRICORN
1980 ARIES / 7.3 TAURUS
1981 AQUARIUS / 28.2 PISCES
1982 CAPRICORN / 4.3 AQUARIUS
1983 PISCES / 23.2 ARIES
1984 SAGITTARIUS /
  25.1 CAPRICORN
1985 ARIES
1986 PISCES / 9.3 ARIES
1987 CAPRICORN
1988 ARIES / 7.3 TAURUS
1989 AQUARIUS / 28.2 PISCES
1990 CAPRICORN / 5.3 AQUARIUS
1991 PISCES / 22.2 ARIES /
  20.3 TAURUS
1992 SAGITTARIUS /
  25.1 CAPRICORN
1993 ARIES
1994 PISCES / 9.3 ARIES
1995 CAPRICORN
1996 ARIES / 7.3 TAURUS
1997 AQUARIUS / 27.2 PISCES
1998 CAPRICORN / 5.3 AQUARIUS
1999 PISCES / 22.2 ARIES /
  19.3 TAURUS
2000 SAGITTARIUS /
  25.1 CAPRICORN
2001 ARIES
2002 PISCES / 9.3 ARIES
2003 CAPRICORN
2004 ARIES / 7.3 TAURUS
2005 AQUARIUS / 27.2 PISCES
2006 CAPRICORN / 5.3 AQUARIUS
2007 PISCES / 22.2 ARIES
2008 SAGITTARIUS /
  25.1 CAPRICORN
2009 ARIES

VENUS THROUGH THE ZODIAC SIGNS

Venus in Aries

Amongst other things, the position of Venus in Aries indicates a fondness for travel, music and all creative pursuits. Your nature tends to be affectionate and you would try not to create confusion or difficulty for others if it could be avoided. Many people with this planetary position have a great love of the theatre, and mental stimulation is of the greatest importance. Early romantic attachments are common with Venus in Aries, so it is very important to establish a genuine sense of romantic continuity. Early marriage is not recommended, especially if it is based on sympathy. You may give your heart a little too readily on occasions.

Venus in Taurus

You are capable of very deep feelings and your emotions tend to last for a very long time. This makes you a trusting partner and lover, whose constancy is second to none. In life you are precise and careful and always try to do things the right way. Although this means an ordered life, which you are comfortable with, it can also lead you to be rather too fussy for your own good. Despite your pleasant nature, you are very fixed in your opinions and quite able to speak your mind. Others are attracted to you and historical astrologers always quoted this position of Venus as being very fortunate in terms of marriage. However, if you find yourself involved in a failed relationship, it could take you a long time to trust again.

Venus in Gemini

As with all associations related to Gemini, you tend to be quite versatile, anxious for change and intelligent in your dealings with the world at large. You may gain money from more than one source but you are equally good at spending it. There is an inference here that you are a good communicator, via either the written or the spoken word, and you love to be in the company of interesting people. Always on the look-out for culture, you may also be very fond of music, and love to indulge the curious and cultured side of your nature. In romance you tend to have more than one relationship and could find yourself associated with someone who has previously been a friend or even a distant relative.

Venus in Cancer

You often stay close to home because you are very fond of family and enjoy many of your most treasured moments when you are with those you love. Being naturally sympathetic, you will always do anything you can to support those around you, even people you hardly know at all. This charitable side of your nature is your most noticeable trait and is one of the reasons why others are naturally so fond of you. Being receptive and in some cases even psychic, you can see through to the soul of most of those with whom you come into contact. You may not commence too many romantic attachments but when you do give your heart, it tends to be unconditionally.

Venus in Leo

It must become quickly obvious to almost anyone you meet that you are kind, sympathetic and yet determined enough to stand up for anyone or anything that is truly important to you. Bright and sunny, you warm the world with your natural enthusiasm and would rarely do anything to hurt those around you, or at least not intentionally. In romance you are ardent and sincere, though some may find your style just a little overpowering. Gains come through your contacts with other people and this could be especially true with regard to romance, for love and money often come hand in hand for those who were born with Venus in Leo. People claim to understand you, though you are more complex than you seem.

Venus in Virgo

Your nature could well be fairly quiet no matter what your Sun sign might be, though this fact often manifests itself as an inner peace and would not prevent you from being basically sociable. Some delays and even the odd disappointment in love cannot be ruled out with this planetary position, though it's a fact that you will usually find the happiness you look for in the end. Catapulting yourself into romantic entanglements that you know to be rather ill-advised is not sensible, and it would be better to wait before you committed yourself exclusively to any one person. It is the essence of your nature to serve the world at large and through doing so it is possible that you will attract money at some stage in your life.

Venus in Libra

Venus is very comfortable in Libra and bestows upon those people who have this planetary position a particular sort of kindness that is easy to recognise. This is a very good position for all sorts of friendships and also for romantic attachments that usually bring much joy into your life. Few individuals with Venus in Libra would avoid marriage and since you are capable of great depths of love, it is likely that you will find a contented personal life. You like to mix with people of integrity and intelligence but don't take kindly to scruffy surroundings or work that means getting your hands too dirty. Careful speculation, good business dealings and money through marriage all seem fairly likely.

Venus in Scorpio

You are quite open and tend to spend money quite freely, even on those occasions when you don't have very much. Although your intentions are always good, there are times when you get yourself in to the odd scrape and this can be particularly true when it comes to romance, which you may come to late or from a rather unexpected direction. Certainly you have the power to be happy and to make others contented on the way, but you find the odd stumbling block on your journey through life and it could seem that you have to work harder than those around you. As a result of this, you gain a much deeper understanding of the true value of personal happiness than many people ever do, and are likely to achieve true contentment in the end.

Venus in Sagittarius

You are lighthearted, cheerful and always able to see the funny side of any situation. These facts enhance your popularity, which is especially high with members of the opposite sex. You should never have to look too far to find romantic interest in your life, though it is just possible that you might be too willing to commit yourself before you are certain that the person in question is right for you. Part of the problem here extends to other areas of life too. The fact is that you like variety in everything and so can tire of situations that fail to offer it. All the same, if you choose wisely and learn to understand your restless side, then great happiness can be yours.

Venus in Capricorn

The most notable trait that comes from Venus in this position is that it makes you trustworthy and able to take on all sorts of responsibilities in life. People are instinctively fond of you and love you all the more because you are always ready to help those who are in any form of need. Social and business popularity can be yours and there is a magnetic quality to your nature that is particularly attractive in a romantic sense. Anyone who wants a partner for a lover, a spouse and a good friend too would almost certainly look in your direction. Constancy is the hallmark of your nature and unfaithfulness would go right against the grain. You might sometimes be a little too trusting.

Venus in Aquarius

This location of Venus offers a fondness for travel and a desire to try out something new at every possible opportunity. You are extremely easy to get along with and tend to have many friends from varied backgrounds, classes and inclinations. You like to live a distinct sort of life and gain a great deal from moving about, both in a career sense and with regard to your home. It is not out of the question that you could form a romantic attachment to someone who comes from far away or be attracted to a person of a distinctly artistic and original nature. What you cannot stand is jealousy, for you have friends of both sexes and would want to keep things that way.

Venus in Pisces

The first thing people tend to notice about you is your wonderful, warm smile. Being very charitable by nature you will do anything to help others, even if you don't know them well. Much of your life may be spent sorting out situations for other people, but it is very important to feel that you are living for yourself too. In the main, you remain cheerful, and tend to be quite attractive to members of the opposite sex. Where romantic attachments are concerned, you could be drawn to people who are significantly older or younger than yourself or to someone with a unique career or point of view. It might be best for you to avoid marrying whilst you are still very young.

THE ASTRAL DIARY

HOW THE DIAGRAMS WORK

Through the picture diagrams in the Astral Diary I want to help you to plot your year. With them you can see where the positive and negative aspects will be found in each month. To make the most of them, all you have to do is remember where and when!

Let me show you how they work ...

THE MONTH AT A GLANCE

Just as there are twelve separate zodiac signs, so astrologers believe that each sign has twelve separate aspects to life. Each of the twelve segments relates to a different personal aspect. I list them all every month so that their meanings are always clear.

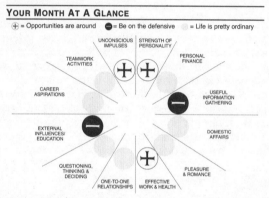

YOUR MONTH AT A GLANCE

⊕ = Opportunities are around   ⊖ = Be on the defensive   = Life is pretty ordinary

UNCONSCIOUS IMPULSES
STRENGTH OF PERSONALITY
TEAMWORK ACTIVITIES
PERSONAL FINANCE
CAREER ASPIRATIONS
USEFUL INFORMATION GATHERING
EXTERNAL INFLUENCES/ EDUCATION
DOMESTIC AFFAIRS
QUESTIONING, THINKING & DECIDING
PLEASURE & ROMANCE
ONE-TO-ONE RELATIONSHIPS
EFFECTIVE WORK & HEALTH

I have designed this chart to show you how and when these twelve different aspects are being influenced throughout the year. When there is a shaded circle, nothing out of the ordinary is to be expected. However, when a circle turns white with a plus sign, the influence is positive. Where the circle is black with a minus sign, it is a negative.

YOUR ENERGY RHYTHM CHART

On the opposite page is a picture diagram in which I am linking your zodiac group to the rhythm of the Moon. In doing this I have calculated when you will be gaining strength from its influence and equally when you may be weakened by it.

If you think of yourself as being like the tides of the ocean then you may understand how your own energies must also rise and fall. And if you understand how it works and when it is working, then you can better organise your activities to achieve more and get things done more easily.

YOUR ENERGY RHYTHM CHART

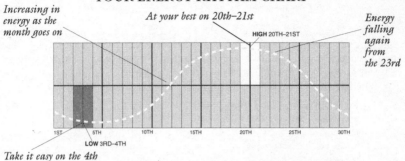

Increasing in energy as the month goes on

At your best on 20th–21st

HIGH 20TH–21ST

Energy falling again from the 23rd

1ST 5TH 10TH 15TH 20TH 25TH 30TH

LOW 3RD–4TH

Take it easy on the 4th

MOVING PICTURE SCREEN
Love, money, career and vitality measured every week

The diagram at the end of each week is designed to be informative and fun. The arrows move up and down the scale to give you an idea of the strength of your opportunities in each area. If LOVE stands at plus 4, then get out and put yourself about because things are going your way in romance! The further down the arrow goes, the weaker the opportunities. Do note that the diagram is an overall view of your astrological aspects and therefore reflects a trend which may not concur with every day in that cycle.

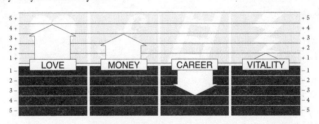

AND FINALLY:

am . . . .

pm . . . .

The two lines that are left blank in each daily entry of the Astral Diary are for your own personal use. You may find them ideal for keeping a check on birthdays or appointments, though it could be an idea to make notes from the astrological trends and diagrams a few weeks in advance. Some of the lines are marked with a key, which indicates the working of astrological cycles in your life. Look out for them each week as they are the best days to take action or make decisions. The daily text tells you which area of your life to focus on.

☿ = Mercury is retrograde on that day.

PISCES: YOUR YEAR IN BRIEF

Although the start of the year might be somewhat quieter than you have been expecting, January and February will at least offer you the chance to take stock and to come to terms with changes that are necessary in your life. Some of these turn out to be extremely positive, especially in the sphere of love, romance and even business. With better luck on your side it looks as though you will be able to turn many situations to your advantage.

As the spring approaches, March and April are going to give you greater energy and offer you new incentives that you probably had not been expecting. That's the hallmark of 2009, and you need to take full advantage of good fortune that comes like a bolt from the blue. You might be less sure at this time what you want to do in terms of your social life, though you instigate most situations rather than simply reacting to them.

May and June could turn out to be extremely fortunate for most sons and daughters of Pisces. What happens at this time is that a great deal of the effort you have put in previously now begins to pay dividends, especially in terms of co-operative ventures. May is especially good in terms of personal attachments, whilst June sees you making new friends right across the board. Some real personalities are likely to be entering your life around this time.

With the high summer, July and August offer even better incentives for travel and bring you closer to your heart's desire in material terms. There are changes to be made in and around your home and it looks as though you will be seeking adventure wherever you go. This is not a time to allow yourself to be stuck in or near your home because you genuinely do need to spread your wings.

The months of September and October might see things slowing down somewhat, or at least that's the way it is going to look at first. Don't take no for an answer at the beginning of September and then you will be back onto the roller coaster once again and getting involved for all you are worth. It is during October that many of the plans you laid much earlier in the year will start to come to fruition.

The final months of 2009, November and December, offer you new incentives in a professional sense and look like keeping up the positive pressure in terms of love and romance. There is a possibility of a new job for some, and different and more stimulating responsibilities for others. The Christmas period may turn out to be especially memorable and it looks as though you will find yourself on the receiving end of surprises that go far beyond what you may have expected. Right at the end of the year you should find almost unbelievable kindness coming from someone.

January 2009

YOUR MONTH AT A GLANCE

⊕ = Opportunities are around ⊖ = Be on the defensive ○ = Life is pretty ordinary

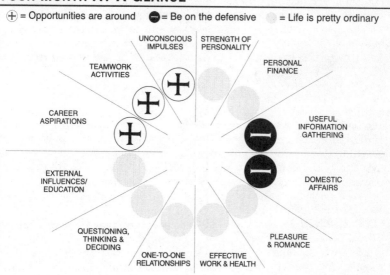

UNCONSCIOUS IMPULSES

STRENGTH OF PERSONALITY

TEAMWORK ACTIVITIES

PERSONAL FINANCE

CAREER ASPIRATIONS

USEFUL INFORMATION GATHERING

EXTERNAL INFLUENCES/ EDUCATION

DOMESTIC AFFAIRS

QUESTIONING, THINKING & DECIDING

PLEASURE & ROMANCE

ONE-TO-ONE RELATIONSHIPS

EFFECTIVE WORK & HEALTH

JANUARY HIGHS AND LOWS

Here I show you how the rhythms of the Moon will affect you this month. Like the tide, your energies and abilities will rise and fall with its pattern. When it is above the centre line, go for it, when it is below, you should be resting. HIGH 2ND–3RD

HIGH 29TH–30TH

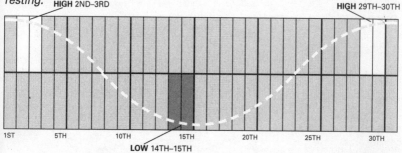

1ST 5TH 10TH 15TH 20TH 25TH 30TH

LOW 14TH–15TH

29 MONDAY
Moon Age Day 2   Moon Sign Capricorn

am . . . .

pm . . . .
Be careful that you don't make impossible demands of others. Maybe you are not thinking things through as clearly as you normally do, or it could be that you are just slightly less sensitive. Your best approach is to look at matters carefully and leave room for flexibility.

30 TUESDAY
Moon Age Day 3   Moon Sign Aquarius

am . . . .

pm . . . .
Once again you can put yourself in the midst of social activities, which you can afford to enjoy a great deal. Part of your mind might still be focused on the future, and you could get somewhat preoccupied so close to the end of the year. Take today for what it's worth and don't get more involved in forward planning than proves to be necessary.

31 WEDNESDAY
Moon Age Day 4   Moon Sign Aquarius

am . . . .

pm . . . .
Once again you have the ability to focus your mind as much on the past as on the future, and as long as you can achieve a sensible balance everything should be fine. By the end of today you may well be reconciled to that same old party or gathering, but you could be quite surprised at the way things eventually pan out.

1 THURSDAY
Moon Age Day 5   Moon Sign Aquarius

am . . . .

pm . . . .
This has potential to be a good start to the year as far as you are concerned because the Moon is moving rapidly towards your own zodiac sign of Pisces. This supports an optimistic approach in which you can look on the bright side for the start of January. Make sure that any hangover is short-lived, and be ready to get a great deal done in these first days.

2 FRIDAY

Moon Age Day 6   Moon Sign Pisces

am . . . .

pm . . . .

Capitalise on the presence of Lady Luck, because the Moon in Pisces is that period of the month known as the lunar high. This assists you to be very positive and allows you to communicate your ideas to others in a very concrete way. A day to welcome new personalities into your life and to make the most of the new and positive ideas they bring.

3 SATURDAY

Moon Age Day 7   Moon Sign Pisces

am . . . .

pm . . . .

You may have to put in some extra effort today, but you can make sure it's worthwhile. Getting ahead of the crowd shouldn't be difficult, and you remain in a good position to influence situations very positively. Affairs of the heart are well accented, and you have what it takes to turn heads, even when you are not trying to do so.

4 SUNDAY

Moon Age Day 8   Moon Sign Aries

am . . . .

pm . . . .

Your thinking today may not be as practical as usual and common sense seems to have gone out of the window in some respects. Your best approach is to check and recheck details carefully in order to avoid delays or disappointments, and to be prepared to deal with anyone around you who seems to be doing all they can to confuse you.

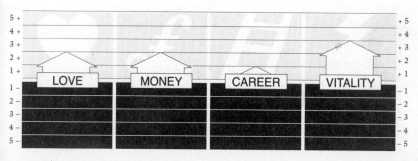

5 MONDAY
Moon Age Day 9   Moon Sign Aries

am . . . .

pm . . . .
Events in your love life can be kept fairly settled at the start of this week, even if you decide to focus much of your attention on your working life. There are new possibilities on offer that could bring greater responsibility but also better financial rewards. It is important to keep your eye on any target you have set yourself.

6 TUESDAY
Moon Age Day 10   Moon Sign Taurus

am . . . .

pm . . . .
There could well be less time for personal luxury at the moment, particularly if you are very busy in a practical sense. It may not occur to you that others have specific needs of you and your natural sensitivity may not be exactly up to scratch. Any delays early in the day can soon be overcome, and progress should be easier towards the evening.

7 WEDNESDAY
Moon Age Day 11   Moon Sign Taurus

am . . . .

pm . . . .
There are good reasons to use today as a cooling-off period as far as romance is concerned, as present trends support a rather strange frame of mind. The accent generally is on the practical side of life and that may not leave much time free to talk to people in the way you normally do. Look out for an interesting new opportunity later in the day.

8 THURSDAY
Moon Age Day 12   Moon Sign Gemini

am . . . .

pm . . . .
Domestic and private interests offer you scope to achieve contentment as the day advances and you have what it takes to turn heads in social situations. There is much to be said for being able to mix business and pleasure, and in any case the sensitive side of your nature can be displayed again – which is how it should be.

9 FRIDAY
Moon Age Day 13   Moon Sign Gemini

am . . . .

pm . . . .
Your social instincts are now emphasised, assisting you to actively seek out interesting company and groups of people who have a similar attitude to life. Now is the time to enjoy yourself, and the end of the working week for many will offer new possibilities that have nothing at all to do with practicalities. In other words, it's time to have fun!

10 SATURDAY
Moon Age Day 14   Moon Sign Cancer

am . . . .

pm . . . .
Allowing your imagination to be stimulated is the order of the day now, and you should be filled with enthusiasm when it comes to doing anything new or even slightly outrageous. No matter what your age, it's worth approaching life like a ten-year-old, and it is this apparent joy that can be so infectious to others. Routines are best avoided today.

11 SUNDAY
Moon Age Day 15   Moon Sign Cancer

am . . . .

pm . . . .
Even if you remain generally cheerful, you might now be more sensitive to slights than would normally be the case. If you believe that people are talking about you, you may also be suspicious regarding what they are saying. Ask yourself whether you are being rather too sensitive for your own good, and remember that a little realism goes a long way.

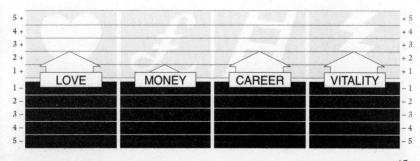

12 MONDAY ☿ *Moon Age Day 16   Moon Sign Leo*

am . . . .

pm . . . .
You now have the ability to create a pleasing impression, no matter what company you keep. This helps you to secure the loyalty of others, and to offer advice where necessary. It should be easy to put yourself into someone else's shoes – after all, empathy is the hallmark of Pisces. Finances could benefit from extra attention this week.

13 TUESDAY ☿ *Moon Age Day 17   Moon Sign Leo*

am . . . .

pm . . . .
Today works best if you develop your own practical goals as much as possible, and although it is important to listen to what colleagues and friends have to say, in the end you need to make up your own mind. Beware of getting involved in discussions that could so easily become rows, and maintain a sense of purpose when tackling new jobs at work.

14 WEDNESDAY ☿ *Moon Age Day 18   Moon Sign Virgo*

am . . . .

pm . . . .
The Moon now moves into Virgo, which is your opposite zodiac sign. This brings that period of the month known as the lunar low. It is at such times that you are encouraged to retreat into yourself a little, and when you may not be on top form socially or romantically. Yours is a complex nature, and you need short periods for reflection.

15 THURSDAY ☿ *Moon Age Day 19   Moon Sign Virgo*

am . . . .

pm . . . .
The lunar low can be a real test of your patience, and how well you do when the chips are down will prove to be very important later on. By all means tackle any jobs you know have to be done, but avoid taking on anything new until you have thought things through properly. Even if others irritate you, reacting too strongly is not advised.

16 FRIDAY ☿ *Moon Age Day 20   Moon Sign Libra*

am . . . .

pm . . . .
There are some unexpected changes on offer. Although the lunar low has now passed, it's worth remaining fairly cautious, especially regarding practical matters. The fact is that trends highlight the jumpy side of your nature rather than your calm and relaxed side. The present position of Mars in your solar chart has much to answer for.

17 SATURDAY ☿ *Moon Age Day 21   Moon Sign Libra*

am . . . .

pm . . . .
The focus is on enhancing your personal life today and getting away from practical issues that can't be resolved in a moment. The weekend offers the chance of fun, particularly if you ditch worries that are both pointless and impossible to address. Stay out there in the social world as much as you can and find new ways to please your partner.

18 SUNDAY ☿ *Moon Age Day 22   Moon Sign Libra*

am . . . .

pm . . . .
You can use your expansive mental outlook to make the most of an exciting time for learning and for getting to grips with situations you have been avoiding. Travel could be on the cards and you may decide that the time is right to make some significant changes in and around your home. Be prepared to offer sound advice to friends who need it.

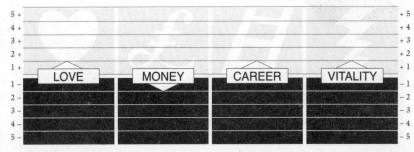

19 MONDAY ☿ *Moon Age Day 23   Moon Sign Scorpio*

am . . . .

pm . . . .
Today is about keeping things on an even keel and doing what you can to pour oil on any troubled waters at home. Even if others seem quite intolerant, your best response is to accept that they may be going through a hard time and offer the support you can. A warm and responsive approach towards your partner can make all the difference now.

20 TUESDAY ☿ *Moon Age Day 24   Moon Sign Scorpio*

am . . . .

pm . . . .
Your imagination may be easily stimulated at this stage, assisting you to see well into the future. Convincing other people that you know what you are talking about may not be very easy, but it might be necessary if you want to get your own way in the longer term. A day to avoid anything you find irritating if at all possible.

21 WEDNESDAY ☿ *Moon Age Day 25   Moon Sign Sagittarius*

am . . . .

pm . . . .
You now have scope to be more relaxed and easy-going. Venus has entered your solar first house and in this position it is very supportive. You can allow your confidence to increase, especially in terms of romance. Any Pisces people who have been looking for a new attachment would be wise to concentrate their efforts around this time.

22 THURSDAY ☿ *Moon Age Day 26   Moon Sign Sagittarius*

am . . . .

pm . . . .
Leadership issues are to the fore under present influences, supporting a strong conviction in your heart that the time is right to assert yourself more. This may surprise others, which is no bad thing, and there isn't much doubt that you can make a solid impression on the world at large. Be prepared for mysterious or odd behaviour from others.

23 FRIDAY
☿   *Moon Age Day 27*   *Moon Sign Sagittarius*

am . . . .

pm . . . .
Romantic relations can now be put under the spotlight, and it looks as though you will have everything you need in order to sweep someone right off their feet. The end of the working week for most Pisces subjects offers a more carefree attitude and a kind of ingenuity that assists you to come up with bright ideas all the time.

24 SATURDAY
☿   *Moon Age Day 28*   *Moon Sign Capricorn*

am . . . .

pm . . . .
The position of the Moon now allows you to bring out the best in yourself and offers you the chance to get back in touch with familiar faces. Maybe these will be former friends you don't see all that often, and if so you could just realise how important these people once were to you. A little nostalgia is no bad thing around this period.

25 SUNDAY
☿   *Moon Age Day 29*   *Moon Sign Capricorn*

am . . . .

pm . . . .
At this time you could have much less thought for what you can get out of situations, particularly if, typical of your zodiac sign, you are committed mainly to helping others. It's a strange fact though that in sacrificing your own needs for the sake of friends, you can often manage to get ahead better than you would if you chose to be selfish.

	LOVE	MONEY	CAREER	VITALITY

26 MONDAY ☿ *Moon Age Day 0   Moon Sign Aquarius*

am . . . .

pm . . . .
Perhaps you need a period that is less demanding at the start of this week.
There are good reasons to avoid too many new responsibilities and to
find ways to put your feet up and relax. In your spare time it is vital that
you pay some attention to your dreams. You may have a chance to turn
at least some of them into realities soon.

27 TUESDAY ☿ *Moon Age Day 1   Moon Sign Aquarius*

am . . . .

pm . . . .
The Sun has now entered your solar twelfth house, supporting a more
emotional phase across the next few weeks. You might also decide on
occasion to withdraw more into your inner world, and to avoid breaking
the bounds of convention. Nevertheless, it's still possible for you to
remain cheerful and committed to family.

28 WEDNESDAY ☿ *Moon Age Day 2   Moon Sign Aquarius*

am . . . .

pm . . . .
Routines can be dealt with easily, though you may feel that it should be
possible to get more from life than you are managing to do at the
moment. Everything today is weighted towards your solar twelfth house,
which offers you greater scope for reflection and an inward-looking
attitude. You can change everything by tomorrow.

29 THURSDAY ☿ *Moon Age Day 3   Moon Sign Pisces*

am . . . .

pm . . . .
As the lunar high arrives, so you have what it takes to be more engaging
in your attitude and to capitalise on your enhanced popularity.
Recognising how much you are loved is the name of the game, and
although a little embarrassment is possible on the way, you have potential
to turn this into one of the best days of the month.

30 FRIDAY ☿ *Moon Age Day 4   Moon Sign Pisces*

am . . . .

pm . . . .

Life should be going with a swing, and as the end of January arrives it looks as though the world can be your oyster. This particular Friday offers the chance to come up with some ingenious notions and to follow them through. If what you are seeking is excitement, the possibility of finding it stands around every new corner, of which there are many!

31 SATURDAY ☿ *Moon Age Day 5   Moon Sign Aries*

am . . . .

pm . . . .

With the lunar high now out of the way, there's nothing wrong with deciding to go with the flow. Even if you can't show quite the ingenuity you did yesterday, you do have the ability to relax and also to engage others. Concern for the underdog is highlighted, allowing you to show your Piscean sensitivity virtually all the time.

1 SUNDAY *Moon Age Day 6   Moon Sign Aries*

am . . . .

pm . . . .

Assistance in terms of your practical goals can be obtained from some surprising directions. Don't turn down the chance to make a favourable impression on people generally, though you also need time for reflection and to examine your own thoughts thoroughly. Routines could seem comfortable, but beware of getting bogged down by them.

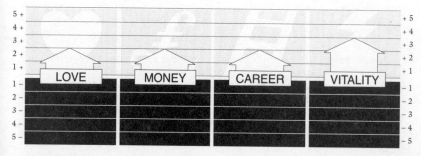

February
2009

YOUR MONTH AT A GLANCE

⊕ = Opportunities are around   ● = Be on the defensive   ○ = Life is pretty ordinary

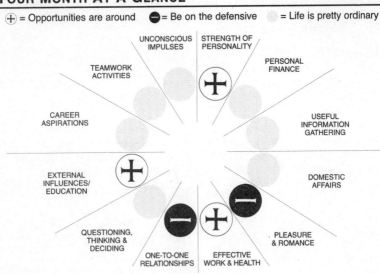

UNCONSCIOUS IMPULSES

STRENGTH OF PERSONALITY

TEAMWORK ACTIVITIES

PERSONAL FINANCE

CAREER ASPIRATIONS

USEFUL INFORMATION GATHERING

EXTERNAL INFLUENCES/ EDUCATION

DOMESTIC AFFAIRS

QUESTIONING, THINKING & DECIDING

ONE-TO-ONE RELATIONSHIPS

EFFECTIVE WORK & HEALTH

PLEASURE & ROMANCE

FEBRUARY HIGHS AND LOWS

Here I show you how the rhythms of the Moon will affect you this month. Like the tide, your energies and abilities will rise and fall with its pattern. When it is above the centre line, go for it, when it is below, you should be resting.

HIGH 25TH–26TH

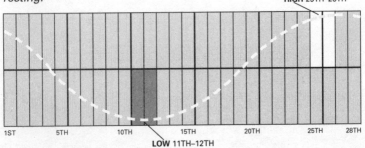

1ST   5TH   10TH   15TH   20TH   25TH   28TH

LOW 11TH–12TH

2 MONDAY
Moon Age Day 7   Moon Sign Taurus

am . . . .

pm . . . .
Things around you assist you to display the best side of your nature. This is as much due to the way you respond to others as it is to anything else. It's time to find out how much your opinions are valued, and you can afford to say a great deal for yourself, especially at work. This can also be a favourable time for educational matters.

3 TUESDAY
Moon Age Day 8   Moon Sign Taurus

am . . . .

pm . . . .
There may well be some unreliable people around at this time, and you would be wise to be very discriminating in the way you approach colleagues. Perhaps it isn't that anyone is trying to cause you problems – it may be just a consequence of their ineptitude. A day to avoid family rows and to play the honest broker whenever you get the chance.

4 WEDNESDAY
Moon Age Day 9   Moon Sign Taurus

am . . . .

pm . . . .
It is towards home and family that you are encouraged to turn your attention at the moment, particularly if the big world outside seems slightly threatening. Also the Moon is in your solar fourth house, doing you few if any favours, and your ability to mix more freely may be limited for now. There are gains to be made in a financial sense.

5 THURSDAY
Moon Age Day 10   Moon Sign Gemini

am . . . .

pm . . . .
Today is all about getting others to understand what you are thinking and explaining yourself to them. Even one definite ally can be worth a great deal, and with their help you can turn ideas into realities. Are you worrying about younger family members? Bear in mind that your worries may well be groundless.

6 FRIDAY

Moon Age Day 11   Moon Sign Gemini

am . . . .

pm . . . .
An over-reflective tendency could now cause you to overlook the need for speed and action. This is something you should avoid because there is progress to be made at the moment. Where any task is concerned it is important to at least try and not to get disheartened before you begin. There is much to be said for being enchanted by romance!

7 SATURDAY

Moon Age Day 12   Moon Sign Cancer

am . . . .

pm . . . .
With Venus now having moved into your solar second house, your appreciation of the material benefits of life should be much enhanced. This isn't very typical for Pisces because for much of the time you live in a more spiritual dimension. There could be an urge at this time to surround yourself with shiny gadgets that you don't really need.

8 SUNDAY

Moon Age Day 13   Moon Sign Cancer

am . . . .

pm . . . .
If you take the opportunity to express your enthusiasm today, that could be worth a great deal to your family and friends. Rather than being too sure of yourself regarding any issue that has caused you some problems in the past, why not seek out the advice of those who definitely do know better? This might include older relatives.

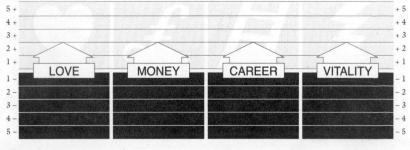

9 MONDAY
Moon Age Day 14   Moon Sign Leo

am . . . .

pm . . . .
Trends encourage you to focus your energies mainly on practical matters at the start of this particular working week, allowing you to gain a good understanding of what makes life work out the way it does. The deeper side of your nature should be on display, and you have a chance to show others how wise and easy-going you can be.

10 TUESDAY
Moon Age Day 15   Moon Sign Leo

am . . . .

pm . . . .
Routines can be dealt with quite easily under prevailing trends, and being satisfied with your lot is the name of the game. This might not extend to relationships, which could be under the spotlight. Some Pisces individuals might be thinking about embarking on a new personal attachment, and may already be looking around.

11 WEDNESDAY
Moon Age Day 16   Moon Sign Virgo

am . . . .

pm . . . .
A state of disorganisation is possible whilst the lunar low is around, though this may be outside your control. By all means do what is necessary, though this isn't an ideal time to get involved in complicated reorganisations. Friday is the day to set your sights on making changes, which for the moment could be quite pointless and very difficult.

12 THURSDAY
Moon Age Day 17   Moon Sign Virgo

am . . . .

pm . . . .
Working slowly and steadily through problems is the way to deal with them now, but even then you may need the timely help and support of your closest allies. It might be difficult to be quite as cheerful and easy-going as usual, particularly if your nature has more 'edge'. If you can get others to understand, they might be prepared to compensate.

13 FRIDAY
Moon Age Day 18   Moon Sign Libra

am . . . .

pm . . . .
Little changes come thick and fast whilst the Moon is in its present position, and you have an opportunity to make life easier for yourself by reorganising as much as you can. This trend is far more likely at work than at home, because in domestic matters you have what it takes to create a settled feeling and a sense of contentment with most things.

14 SATURDAY
Moon Age Day 19   Moon Sign Libra

am . . . .

pm . . . .
There is now a tendency to ignore responsibilities in favour of doing whatever takes your fancy. Today is also about having plenty to say for yourself, which is fine just as long as you have what it takes to back up your boasts. Even if this is the case in the main, bear in mind that there might be occasions when you come decidedly unstuck.

15 SUNDAY
Moon Age Day 20   Moon Sign Scorpio

am . . . .

pm . . . .
What a great day this would be for outdoor pursuits. You needn't let the winter weather dampen your spirits, and a good long walk could be just what the doctor ordered. Make the most of the chance to find some place where there is little artificial noise but plenty of elemental power – something that Pisces understands well.

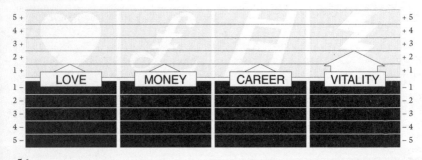

16 MONDAY
Moon Age Day 21   Moon Sign Scorpio

am . . . .

pm . . . .
You would be wise to avoid risky speculations for the moment and, in a
financial sense at least, to stick to what you know and understand well.
Remember that for every sudden gain when it comes to money, rapid
losses are also possible. It might be better to hold tight to what you have
for the moment and to stay off the roller coaster.

17 TUESDAY
Moon Age Day 22   Moon Sign Scorpio

am . . . .

pm . . . .
You might have a hard time being clear-headed for the moment. This is
because the Sun is still in your solar twelfth house and doesn't move away
from it for three or four more days. Some of your thoughts and ideas
could prove to be quite misleading, and there is much to be said for
analysing situations very carefully before making up your mind.

18 WEDNESDAY
Moon Age Day 23   Moon Sign Sagittarius

am . . . .

pm . . . .
Right now you might feel like transcending anything that is totally
normal and sailing off on a flight of fancy. That's all well and good, but
it doesn't get the washing-up done, and it won't earn you any money
either. Now is the time to concentrate on the practical side of life, which
could turn out to be far more interesting than you expected.

19 THURSDAY
Moon Age Day 24   Moon Sign Sagittarius

am . . . .

pm . . . .
The Sun enters your solar first house today, offering you scope to begin
a new cycle. Make the most of a positive interlude and the chance to take
a more focused approach generally. You can also display the power of
your personality more than has been the case across the last few weeks,
and this will assist you to shine when in company.

20 FRIDAY
Moon Age Day 25   Moon Sign Capricorn

am . . . .

pm . . . .
Trends suggest that some of your desires may be a little exaggerated and that you won't be entirely realistic in the way you look at life. This could lead to flights of fancy, though there is nothing wrong with these as long as you recognise them for what they are. When the chips are down you need to be more practical, and that should be possible now.

21 SATURDAY
Moon Age Day 26   Moon Sign Capricorn

am . . . .

pm . . . .
The emphasis is now more strongly on your social life than it has been for quite some time. Rather than locking yourself away in your own little shell, why not get yourself out into the social mainstream? You can be the life and soul of any party that is taking place this weekend, and may even decide to host one yourself!

22 SUNDAY
Moon Age Day 27   Moon Sign Capricorn

am . . . .

pm . . . .
Think about your current ambitions and ideals. Are they enough? It's natural to want something more from life, and to want it as quickly as possible. Pisces is on the move, and there may be so many things happening around you that it is difficult to keep up, and even more awkward trying to choose the best course of action.

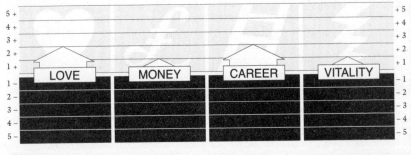

23 MONDAY
Moon Age Day 28   Moon Sign Aquarius

am . . . .

pm . . . .
It's worth keeping abreast of responsibilities just for the moment because there should be plenty of time to do what you want in due course. If you keep your eye on the ball in a practical and a career sense, you will not regret having done so later. If you show people just how capable you can be, new responsibilities could be there for the taking.

24 TUESDAY
Moon Age Day 29   Moon Sign Aquarius

am . . . .

pm . . . .
This is a time for reflection and creativity in equal amounts. You should know what looks and feels right, and can use this knowledge to present yourself to the world in a very positive manner. Beware of being too secretive regarding your love life. If those around you become too curious, they might decide to 'dig' more than you would wish.

25 WEDNESDAY
Moon Age Day 0   Moon Sign Pisces

am . . . .

pm . . . .
A day to get an early start and then get busy. The lunar high could not come at a more fortunate time for you. The Sun is positively placed in your chart and there is a greater incentive to get on well across the board than has been present since the beginning of the year. An ideal time to contact people you don't see often, and to make the most of their company.

26 THURSDAY
Moon Age Day 1   Moon Sign Pisces

am . . . .

pm . . . .
Plans and schemes now receive an extra boost, so do take advantage of the fact. If you feel you need more excitement in your life, remember that this comes in many different forms. Maybe you are in the mood for a complete change of scene, and life itself could offer you the very best opportunity to make some quite significant alterations.

27 FRIDAY
Moon Age Day 2   Moon Sign Aries

am . . . .

pm . . . .
It's a fact that some pleasures could turn out to be very expensive, though in reality the best times of all come completely free of charge. You now have scope to gain plenty of support for your new ideas, which could well be coming thick and fast at this time. Rather than getting too hung up on details now, be ready to look to the bigger picture.

28 SATURDAY
Moon Age Day 3   Moon Sign Aries

am . . . .

pm . . . .
You can afford to let yourself go and enjoy whatever you happen to be doing at any particular time. You needn't worry too much about consequences, particularly if you allow others to make some of the running. Bear in mind that you can't be in charge of everything, and there is much to be said for trusting those around you to make certain decisions.

1 SUNDAY
Moon Age Day 4   Moon Sign Aries

am . . . .

pm . . . .
The emphasis is on a desire for greater movement and the chance to spread your wings, especially when it comes to your personal life. Some Pisces subjects will be embarking on new relationships around now, but only time will tell if you have chosen wisely. Why not look to family members for entertainment – and even some comedy?

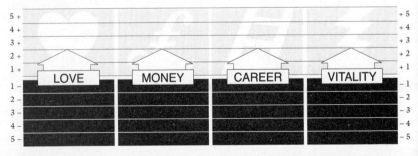

March 2009

YOUR MONTH AT A GLANCE

⊕ = Opportunities are around   ⊖ = Be on the defensive   ⊙ = Life is pretty ordinary

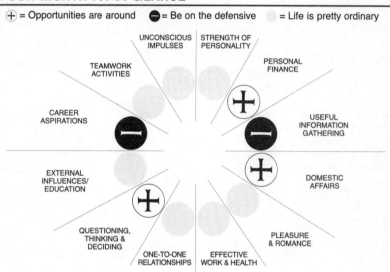

MARCH HIGHS AND LOWS

Here I show you how the rhythms of the Moon will affect you this month. Like the tide, your energies and abilities will rise and fall with its pattern. When it is above the centre line, go for it, when it is below, you should be resting.

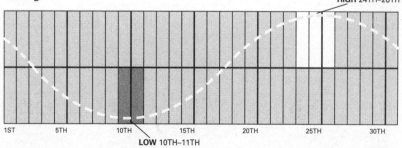

HIGH 24TH–26TH

1ST   5TH   10TH   15TH   20TH   25TH   30TH

LOW 10TH–11TH

2 MONDAY
Moon Age Day 5   Moon Sign Taurus

am . . . .

pm . . . .
Some planets, for example Mercury, refuse to leave their twelfth-house position for the moment, and this can still cause you a problem or two. It might be hard to commit yourself absolutely to the changes you know are necessary and there could be a tendency to hang onto the past, especially when it comes to the way you are talking.

3 TUESDAY
Moon Age Day 6   Moon Sign Taurus

am . . . .

pm . . . .
Despite a few niggles, you are now in a position to commit yourself to a new way of looking at your life. You can afford to show great self-confidence in your work – or in education if you are at school or university. Today is about impressing others with your common sense, while still getting them to recognise the depth of your Pisces nature.

4 WEDNESDAY
Moon Age Day 7   Moon Sign Gemini

am . . . .

pm . . . .
Make the most of your ability to have a greater influence on events and to make more of the decisions that have a bearing on your life. From a financial point of view it is important to live within your means, though it's possible to take the odd chance and get away with it. You would be wise to use your intuition when it comes to assessing strangers.

5 THURSDAY
Moon Age Day 8   Moon Sign Gemini

am . . . .

pm . . . .
A day to enjoy being on the move and to refuse to have your wings clipped by anyone. Between now and the far end of the upcoming weekend the emphasis is on your desire to embark on some sort of journey. What's more, you have what it takes to make your wishes come true.

6 FRIDAY
Moon Age Day 9   Moon Sign Cancer

am . . . .

pm . . . .
You can allow your sense of optimism to grow by the moment, particularly if others generally seem to be doing all they can to make you happy. If you feel slightly hemmed in by circumstances, it is now up to you to do something about it. For a start, you can refuse to get involved in pointless discussions or arguments.

7 SATURDAY
Moon Age Day 10   Moon Sign Cancer

am . . . .

pm . . . .
If it feels as though there is something missing today, it is up to you to paint the picture of your life yourself. Don't rely too much on what other people say they are going to do because this is a time for actions rather than words. Once you manage to get everyone moving, you can persuade them to follow your lead.

8 SUNDAY
Moon Age Day 11   Moon Sign Leo

am . . . .

pm . . . .
This would be an ideal time to focus on money and to examine very carefully all your financial circumstances. Of course everyone would like to be better off than they are, but you need to consider whether you are spending unnecessarily. When it comes to romance, you now have all the right words and gestures to impress someone.

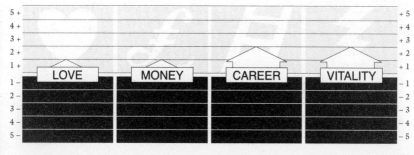

9 MONDAY
Moon Age Day 12   Moon Sign Leo

am . . . .

pm . . . .
The possibility of going head to head with someone today means you would be wise to be on your mettle. It is important to be sure of your facts, particularly if you are planning to embark on any sort of serious discussion. At home your interests are best served if you remain warm, receptive and eager to please just about everyone in your family.

10 TUESDAY
Moon Age Day 13   Moon Sign Virgo

am . . . .

pm . . . .
Frustrations are possible when it comes to getting things accomplished in the way you would wish, thanks to the lunar low. There are some gains to be made in terms of money, but some of your victories could be hollow ones unless you remain focused and definite in your opinions. There isn't really any room for doubt under present trends.

11 WEDNESDAY
Moon Age Day 14   Moon Sign Virgo

am . . . .

pm . . . .
Even if things still don't look too good in a general sense, remember that with the lunar low around, you are lucky to be making any progress at all. Why not turn your attention to things you actually want to do, instead of taking on board too many responsibilities? It's worth letting other people do some of the hard work while you find ways to relax.

12 THURSDAY
Moon Age Day 15   Moon Sign Libra

am . . . .

pm . . . .
Now you get the chance to sharpen up your instincts and to use your intuition to the full. There are gains to be made in a professional sense, and you also have scope to calm things down somewhat at home. You can capitalise on better luck, and it looks as though you will be in a position to back your hunches much more than of late.

13 FRIDAY
Moon Age Day 16   Moon Sign Libra

am . . . .

pm . . . .
Don't be afraid to assume a leading role today. With the Sun in its present position and the Moon also on your side, you can get others to listen to what you have to say and to follow your instructions to the letter. Make the most of this stimulating and action-packed period by being willing to take on much more than has been the case for a week or so.

14 SATURDAY
Moon Age Day 17   Moon Sign Libra

am . . . .

pm . . . .
This is a day for thinking, and a time when your innermost musings should be not only accurate but also quite inspirational. You can get everyone to love you now, particularly if you show your natural kindness and your ability to help in practical ways. The only slight caution relates to taking on only those tasks you know you can complete.

15 SUNDAY
Moon Age Day 18   Moon Sign Scorpio

am . . . .

pm . . . .
In a financial sense you can strengthen your position at the moment – even if you don't realise at first that you are doing it. This makes today an ideal time to get to the shops and seek out some real bargains, though you will probably need some patience. Why not take a good friend with you and shop until you drop? Romance is also well accented from today.

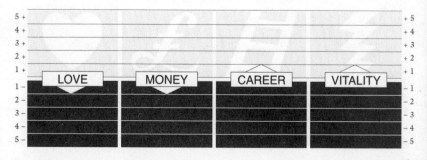

16 MONDAY
Moon Age Day 19   Moon Sign Scorpio

am . . . .

pm . . . .
If you have an enemy at the moment it could be your temper. Mars is in your solar first house, which can be very positive in most respects. But it can encourage you to be quite tetchy and inclined to shoot from the hip. There are occasions at the moment when it would be far better to count to ten before you respond – that way you won't feel bad later.

17 TUESDAY
Moon Age Day 20   Moon Sign Sagittarius

am . . . .

pm . . . .
Trends now emphasise vitality, so capitalise on the energy you have available, and on opportunities to pursue success. The focus is on your ability to get things to fall into place and to use your sense of purpose to the full. As far as personal attachments are concerned you seem to have everything you need to make an important conquest.

18 WEDNESDAY
Moon Age Day 21   Moon Sign Sagittarius

am . . . .

pm . . . .
Around now yours can be a very versatile zodiac sign. Now is the time to get cracking with new ideas and to wring every possible drop of luck out of most situations. If you show that you are keen to become involved in life, you should be able to increase your popularity too, because there's no doubt about it – you can get people to notice you.

19 THURSDAY
Moon Age Day 22   Moon Sign Capricorn

am . . . .

pm . . . .
Be prepared to deal with some opposition to your schemes today, and to talk constantly if you want others to follow your lead. Fortunately you are in a position to use your sense of humour and to pass it on to others. It's a fact that at the moment this may well get you much further than arguing or losing your temper.

20 FRIDAY
Moon Age Day 23   Moon Sign Capricorn

am . . . .

pm . . . .
The potential for monetary gain is now likely to be better than it has been. However, even if you can attract money from various different directions, you may well be spending cash almost as quickly as it comes in. Family matters need careful consideration, especially if someone younger wants to do something about which you have serious doubts.

21 SATURDAY
Moon Age Day 24   Moon Sign Capricorn

am . . . .

pm . . . .
Today is ideal for concentrating on private or emotional issues, and you can afford to spend quite a lot of time mulling things over, particularly if decisions are hard to come by. Conforming to the expectations of others, even those of your partner, can be difficult, and you may first have to convince yourself that what they want you to do is necessary.

22 SUNDAY
Moon Age Day 25   Moon Sign Aquarius

am . . . .

pm . . . .
Your powers of attraction have rarely been stronger than they are now, so if there is someone you want to impress and who you really fancy, now is the time to strut your stuff! Even if keeping up with changing trends and fashions isn't usually your thing, today offers you scope to explore such matters, and to bring the stylish side of your personality to the fore.

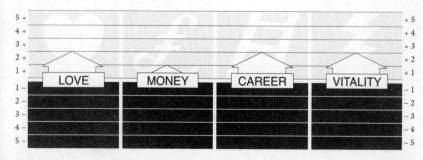

23 MONDAY
Moon Age Day 26   Moon Sign Aquarius

am . . . .

pm . . . .
This would be a good time to weigh up the pros and cons of any business venture. You should also be in a good position to convince others that your point of view is sound and that you know what you are doing. The fact that you might not be half as confident as you appear has little or nothing to do with the eventual outcome.

24 TUESDAY
Moon Age Day 27   Moon Sign Pisces

am . . . .

pm . . . .
Everything comes to he or she who is willing to wait – and your time can be right now! The lunar high boosts your spirits, assisting you in company and helping you to achieve a high degree of popularity. This, together with your natural ability to choose the right course of action, gives you everything you need to make this a successful and happy day.

25 WEDNESDAY
Moon Age Day 28   Moon Sign Pisces

am . . . .

pm . . . .
Ambitions are now honed to perfection and you have what it takes to move forward progressively in life. Most important of all is the way you make use of your magnetic personality. It's always that way, but for some of the time you are inclined to hide your light under a bushel. Now is the time to shine like a star and make sure everyone notices.

26 THURSDAY
Moon Age Day 0   Moon Sign Pisces

am . . . .

pm . . . .
The lunar high is still around, at least for the first part of the day. But situations of confrontation are still a distinct possibility, and a careful approach works best. Mars remains in your solar first house, supporting a more volatile tendency than would usually be the case. There's nothing wrong with wanting things 'just so', especially at home.

27 FRIDAY

Moon Age Day 1   Moon Sign Aries

am . . . .

pm . . . .
There are new ways to communicate and a better ability to get on well with people who have given you problems in the past. This is certainly no time to argue for your limitations, and you need to be ready to act at all times. No astrologer would describe the average Piscean as being like a coiled spring, but you can certainly be one now!

28 SATURDAY

Moon Age Day 2   Moon Sign Aries

am . . . .

pm . . . .
You can now take constructive actions that will have a strong bearing on your financial situation weeks and months down the road. From a social point of view today is ideal for enjoying the cut and thrust of a busy life and for seeking opportunities to meet new people. New activities could hold a special interest for you around now.

29 SUNDAY

Moon Age Day 3   Moon Sign Taurus

am . . . .

pm . . . .
This is a good time to get things done quickly, offering you scope to make almost any task go swimmingly and avoid getting bogged down by doing the same thing for hours on end. The emphasis is now on finding as much variety as possible and on seeking out the company of people you find interesting, intelligent and stimulating.

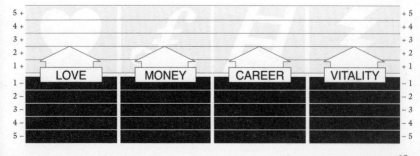

30 MONDAY   *Moon Age Day 4   Moon Sign Taurus*

am . . . .

pm . . . .
The Sun is now in your solar second house and this turns out to be first
rate for practical ideas and for planning at work. If you are between jobs
at the moment, it's worth concentrating your efforts around this time
and pursuing opportunities in various different directions. Be prepared to
listen to what others are telling you this evening.

31 TUESDAY   *Moon Age Day 5   Moon Sign Gemini*

am . . . .

pm . . . .
Success and financial growth are both legacies of a second-house Venus,
which also assists you to increase your attractiveness and make contact
with people who find you fascinating. If all of this seems exciting, it should
do, particularly if you are determined to give of your best and show people
what you are capable of being. In reality you are being yourself.

1 WEDNESDAY   *Moon Age Day 6   Moon Sign Gemini*

am . . . .

pm . . . .
You now have what it takes to make the best of domestic matters, especially
in terms of people who can be a little difficult to deal with at times. Make
full use of your present ability to charm the birds down from the trees and
also to get people to do your bidding without trying too hard.

2 THURSDAY   *Moon Age Day 7   Moon Sign Cancer*

am . . . .

pm . . . .
The competitive spirit you possess generally brings out the best in you –
that is when you are not getting paranoid and retreating into your shell.
You needn't let that happen at the moment. If you show how confident
you are, that's all it should take for others to follow your lead. Get ready
to welcome new personalities into your life now.

3 FRIDAY

Moon Age Day 8   Moon Sign Cancer

am . . . .

pm . . . .
Focus on your social life and upon your present sense of freedom and you shouldn't go far wrong. On the other hand, if you allow yourself to be tied down by responsibilities or the obligations you feel towards other people, life could seem quite tedious. The choice is yours, so why not shelve those pointless worries and find ways to have fun?

4 SATURDAY

Moon Age Day 9   Moon Sign Leo

am . . . .

pm . . . .
An ideal day to enhance your finances and to think up ingenious ways to please people. This is Pisces at its best, and you can afford to devote plenty of energy offering the sort of assistance for which you are justifiably famous. You might be especially sympathetic to people who are having personal problems of some sort.

5 SUNDAY

Moon Age Day 10   Moon Sign Leo

am . . . .

pm . . . .
Even if you feel powerful and buoyed up with energy, beware of wearing yourself out chasing rainbows. Make sure that what you do is worthwhile and that it will increase your standing in society somehow. The way other people see you now and across the next couple of weeks could turn out to be far more important than you might expect.

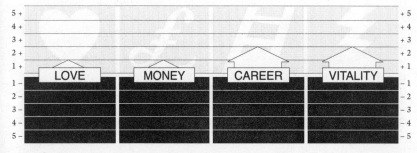

April 2009

YOUR MONTH AT A GLANCE

⊕ = Opportunities are around   ⊖ = Be on the defensive   = Life is pretty ordinary

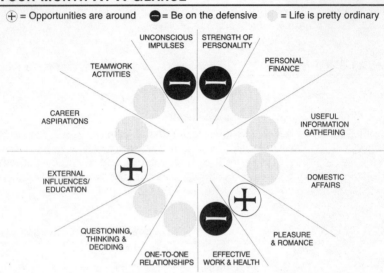

UNCONSCIOUS IMPULSES

STRENGTH OF PERSONALITY

PERSONAL FINANCE

TEAMWORK ACTIVITIES

CAREER ASPIRATIONS

USEFUL INFORMATION GATHERING

EXTERNAL INFLUENCES/ EDUCATION

DOMESTIC AFFAIRS

QUESTIONING, THINKING & DECIDING

ONE-TO-ONE RELATIONSHIPS

EFFECTIVE WORK & HEALTH

PLEASURE & ROMANCE

APRIL HIGHS AND LOWS

Here I show you how the rhythms of the Moon will affect you this month. Like the tide, your energies and abilities will rise and fall with its pattern. When it is above the centre line, go for it, when it is below, you should be resting.

HIGH 21ST–22ND

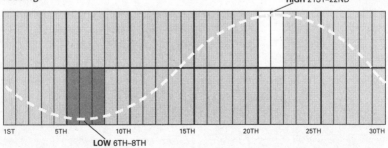

1ST   5TH   10TH   15TH   20TH   25TH   30TH

LOW 6TH–8TH

6 MONDAY
Moon Age Day 11   Moon Sign Virgo

am . . . .

pm . . . .
You might decide you are better off taking life slightly easy today. The lunar low may well take the wind out of your sails when it comes to practical jobs, and it could feel as though you simply can't get yourself going in the way you would wish. On a more personal footing, the time could be right for a serious but useful talk with your partner.

7 TUESDAY
Moon Age Day 12   Moon Sign Virgo

am . . . .

pm . . . .
If you feel held back or frustrated in some way, take courage from the fact that the lunar low will be out of the way by tomorrow. If you concentrate on those matters that really need sorting out and avoid complicating things, all should be well. It is even possible that you can use today to strengthen your financial position, perhaps in an unexpected way.

8 WEDNESDAY
Moon Age Day 13   Moon Sign Virgo

am . . . .

pm . . . .
Trends support a special interest in innovative ideas, and you can get ahead by using your imagination as much as your common sense. You have the ability to see things that others can't, and could turn your instincts to your advantage on more than one occasion. When it comes to certain tasks today, don't be afraid to admit that you do need help.

9 THURSDAY
Moon Age Day 14   Moon Sign Libra

am . . . .

pm . . . .
Your financial progress looks better again, and you may be able to capitalise more on April than on most months so far this year. There could be a change in responsibilities around this time, and some Pisces subjects might also be thinking seriously about a career change. Your popularity in a social sense assists you to be number one all round.

10 FRIDAY
Moon Age Day 15   Moon Sign Libra

am . . . .

pm . . . .
Some people might consider you to be a bit of a gossip at the moment, even if from your point of perspective you are simply remaining interested and being friendly. All the same it is possible that you could inadvertently upset someone with your remarks, and you do need to be fairly sure of your facts before you spill the beans to anyone.

11 SATURDAY
Moon Age Day 16   Moon Sign Scorpio

am . . . .

pm . . . .
When it comes to a sense of personal freedom, today is very important. This is the time to expand your personal horizons and to stand up for what you believe is right for you. Remember that in your own life, it's your opinions that count. It's worth asking yourself whether those who can't accept this should fade into the background.

12 SUNDAY
Moon Age Day 17   Moon Sign Scorpio

am . . . .

pm . . . .
Your romantic life can be central today. Venus is now back in your solar first house and from this position it encourages a more amorous approach in which you are more inclined to speak about the way you feel. This is definitely no time to be a shrinking violet, and you need leave nobody in any doubt where your affections lie.

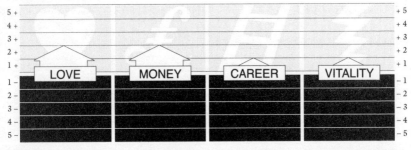

13 MONDAY

Moon Age Day 18   Moon Sign Sagittarius

am . . . .

pm . . . .
The changeable side of your nature is highlighted, emphasising an urge
to be constantly on the move. Even if there are circumstances that keep
you in one place, there's nothing wrong with fighting against these
whenever you can, and you can afford to make it plain to everyone that
you don't want to feel restricted in any way.

14 TUESDAY

Moon Age Day 19   Moon Sign Sagittarius

am . . . .

pm . . . .
Current personal development becomes even more important as the days
pass. Prepare to look for opportunities to get ahead in life and to make
the sort of changes your instincts tell you are necessary. It's time to take
the initiative and to make sure that everyone knows exactly what you
want. The help you can get from friends can make all the difference.

15 WEDNESDAY

Moon Age Day 20   Moon Sign Sagittarius

am . . . .

pm . . . .
The spotlight is on a strong argumentative quality today, particularly if
people or circumstances prevent you from getting what you know is
rightfully yours. Most of your time could be spent sorting things out for
other people, though at the moment a slightly more selfish tendency may
be apparent, which is quite understandable.

16 THURSDAY

Moon Age Day 21   Moon Sign Capricorn

am . . . .

pm . . . .
If you want to secure a tidy profit in something you are presently
undertaking, your best approach is to be ready to move fairly quickly.
Current trends are generally favourable, and you can use this interlude to
make some progress for yourself, whilst at the same time attending to the
needs of others, including family members.

17 FRIDAY   *Moon Age Day 22   Moon Sign Capricorn*

am . . . .

pm . . . .
You have scope to be quite fortunate in partnerships of any sort, and you can make the most of this influence in any dealings you have with awkward types today. Venus remains in your solar first house, which should be a positive trend when it comes to romance. Maybe a better understanding between yourself and your partner is possible.

18 SATURDAY   *Moon Age Day 23   Moon Sign Aquarius*

am . . . .

pm . . . .
Even if there is a great deal of demand on your energies at this time, you might still be tempted to fit in so many things that you make yourself dizzy in hindsight. If you do have a few moments to spare you can afford to withdraw into that private little world of the Piscean, which is absolutely essential to your long-term well-being.

19 SUNDAY   *Moon Age Day 24   Moon Sign Aquarius*

am . . . .

pm . . . .
There are signs that what you say could be misinterpreted by others at the moment, which makes it especially crucial that you choose your words wisely and make sure everyone understands you fully. Remember that projecting yourself too forcefully can be counterproductive, particularly if you manage to alienate those around you as a result.

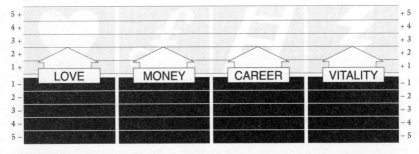

20 MONDAY
Moon Age Day 25   Moon Sign Aquarius

am . . . .

pm . . . .
By tomorrow the lunar high will be with you, which is why it would be sensible today to clear the decks for action. This is not the ideal time to take any major decisions, thanks to the position of the Moon. However, there are good reasons to use this interlude to decide how you want to proceed and to get yourself ready.

21 TUESDAY
Moon Age Day 26   Moon Sign Pisces

am . . . .

pm . . . .
This is a day on which you can make a great success of brand new interests. Your personal power and effectiveness knows no bounds, and the power of the lunar high encourages you to get yourself noticed. This would be a great time to get away from routines, and if you have planned any journey for today, so much the better.

22 WEDNESDAY
Moon Age Day 27   Moon Sign Pisces

am . . . .

pm . . . .
You are now in the midst of a high-energy trend and should be ready to make the most of any opportunity that comes your way. There is much to be said for taking the odd risk and showing yourself to be quite positive in your attitude towards any sphere of your life. Stand by to reap the rewards offered by new personalities you bring into your life now.

23 THURSDAY
Moon Age Day 28   Moon Sign Aries

am . . . .

pm . . . .
Communication issues are favourably highlighted under present trends, which may be all you need to help you talk the hind leg off a donkey! Someone or something may put you in the picture regarding a current ambition, and could make it possible for you to give of your best. If standard responses don't work in matters of love, why not be original?

24 FRIDAY
Moon Age Day 29   Moon Sign Aries

am . . . .

pm . . . .
Impractical or pointless expenditure could well be a feature of the current situation, so all things considered you would be wise to hold onto your resources for the moment. Today is about being careful before you expand your horizons too much, because measured progress is the key at present. Too much advancement could lead to mistakes.

25 SATURDAY
Moon Age Day 0   Moon Sign Taurus

am . . . .

pm . . . .
You now have scope to enliven the atmosphere by just being yourself. If you show your kind and considerate side, people should love to have you around, and you might also have a chance to display your common sense. Trends also highlight new sights and sounds, as well as moments of special 'oneness' with those you love the most.

26 SUNDAY
Moon Age Day 1   Moon Sign Taurus

am . . . .

pm . . . .
Your curiosity and thirst for knowledge knows no bounds at the moment. There are a number of planetary positions contributing to your sense of wonder and assisting you throughout most of today in any sort of search you decide to conduct. If you have meetings to attend or are simply getting together with friends, make sure you have a good time.

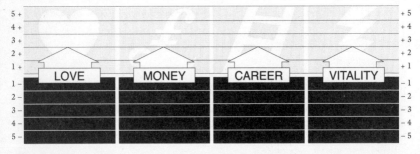

27 MONDAY   *Moon Age Day 2   Moon Sign Gemini*

am . . . .

pm . . . .
Although your financial situation may be up and down at the moment,
that shouldn't stop you finding ways to make more money, even if some
of these are for the future. Ask yourself whether being in too much of a
hurry in practical situations is the best way to get results. Would a little
patience work a great deal better?

28 TUESDAY   *Moon Age Day 3   Moon Sign Gemini*

am . . . .

pm . . . .
The emphasis is now on how rewarding your home life can be, and you
could well be in a prime position to help someone with a problem that
seems insurmountable to them but easy to solve as far as you are
concerned. This is a time to complete projects and to get ready for new
situations that are available to you throughout May – and far beyond.

29 WEDNESDAY   *Moon Age Day 4   Moon Sign Cancer*

am . . . .

pm . . . .
The Sun has now moved into your solar third house. This helps to
enhance your ability to communicate with the world at large, though it
might also support a feeling of restlessness and an inclination to move
around. There are gains to be made by contacting people you haven't
seen for ages, by whatever method of communication works best.

30 THURSDAY   *Moon Age Day 5   Moon Sign Cancer*

am . . . .

pm . . . .
Enjoying yourself and having fun may be very important at the moment,
but you would also be wise to put in the necessary hours to be certain
you have everything you need fully sorted out. A favourable day to
combine work and leisure, and to make friends out of those who have
previously been little more than acquaintances.

1 FRIDAY

Moon Age Day 6   Moon Sign Cancer

am . . . .

pm . . . .
It's the first day of May and an ideal time to get organised. High spirits
are the order of the day, and you can tap into plenty of energy when you
need it the most. Not everyone might be on your side, especially when it
comes to some of your more original or peculiar notions, but if you
remain good humoured you might talk some people round.

2 SATURDAY

Moon Age Day 7   Moon Sign Leo

am . . . .

pm . . . .
Getting your message across to others is now even more important than
it was yesterday. You can use the weekend to achieve longed-for
objectives, and to move in circles away from your house, your street or
even your town if you get the chance. It doesn't matter how you achieve
it, but what matters at this time is making contact.

3 SUNDAY

Moon Age Day 8   Moon Sign Leo

am . . . .

pm . . . .
Today is about feeling comfortable with your lot in life generally, and
you seem to have what it takes to get your own way, especially in your
home environment. You may decide to settle back and allow others to
take the strain, which with the lunar low approaching could be the best
way to proceed.

	LOVE		MONEY		CAREER		VITALITY	
5 +									+ 5
4 +									+ 4
3 +									+ 3
2 +									+ 2
1 +									+ 1
1 −									− 1
2 −									− 2
3 −									− 3
4 −									− 4
5 −									− 5

May 2009

YOUR MONTH AT A GLANCE

$\oplus$ = Opportunities are around $\ominus$ = Be on the defensive   = Life is pretty ordinary

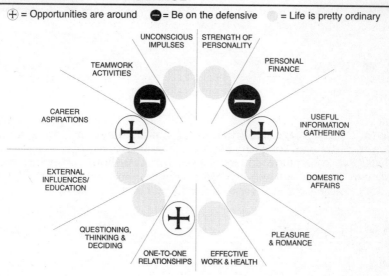

UNCONSCIOUS IMPULSES

STRENGTH OF PERSONALITY

TEAMWORK ACTIVITIES

PERSONAL FINANCE

CAREER ASPIRATIONS

USEFUL INFORMATION GATHERING

EXTERNAL INFLUENCES/ EDUCATION

DOMESTIC AFFAIRS

QUESTIONING, THINKING & DECIDING

PLEASURE & ROMANCE

ONE-TO-ONE RELATIONSHIPS

EFFECTIVE WORK & HEALTH

MAY HIGHS AND LOWS

Here I show you how the rhythms of the Moon will affect you this month. Like the tide, your energies and abilities will rise and fall with its pattern. When it is above the centre line, go for it, when it is below, you should be resting.

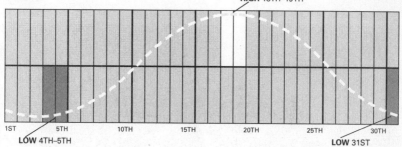

HIGH 18TH–19TH

1ST   5TH   10TH   15TH   20TH   25TH   30TH

LOW 4TH–5TH

LOW 31ST

4 MONDAY
Moon Age Day 9   Moon Sign Virgo

am . . . .

pm . . . .
Today the lunar low is inclined to hold you back somewhat, or at least that is how it feels. In reality you have some very strong supporting planets around you at the moment. The Sun assists you in your attempts to explain yourself to others, and you have what it takes to prepare for what could be a hectic period to come.

5 TUESDAY
Moon Age Day 10   Moon Sign Virgo

am . . . .

pm . . . .
Constructive and realistic thinking might be best kept to a minimum. This is not because anything in particular is going wrong but more on account of your desire to retreat from the world into your own little universe. If there is plenty going on around you, this trend could be short-lived, and may not even survive for the whole of today.

6 WEDNESDAY
Moon Age Day 11   Moon Sign Libra

am . . . .

pm . . . .
Once again it is the way you come across to others that counts most. Your looks, your attitude and your ability to say the right thing will all be important when it comes to getting ahead. The focus is on being more ambitious than is sometimes the case, and you might even surprise colleagues and friends with the way you carry yourself now.

7 THURSDAY
☿   *Moon Age Day 12   Moon Sign Libra*

am . . . .

pm . . . .
Home and family could be of supreme importance at this time, encouraging you to expend much of your energy on making your nearest and dearest happy. This should not be too difficult as far as matters of love are concerned, because you have what it takes to charm the very birds down from the trees. Who could resist your winning ways?

8 FRIDAY
☿   *Moon Age Day 13*   *Moon Sign Scorpio*

am . . . .

pm . . . .
Travel could offer some very definite benefits as the weekend approaches, and those Pisces subjects who have chosen this time to take a holiday will probably have made a most fortunate decision. There are good reasons to keep abreast of news and views in your vicinity, and to take this opportunity to get to grips with issues you see as important.

9 SATURDAY
☿   *Moon Age Day 14*   *Moon Sign Scorpio*

am . . . .

pm . . . .
Impetuosity is the name of the game today, and although that can make for a fun time it also means that the odd gaffe is possible. You needn't let this bother you too much, because you should be happy to be yourself and to make the most of whatever life has to offer. The weekend isn't the ideal time for routines, and pursuing change can work wonders now.

10 SUNDAY
☿   *Moon Age Day 15*   *Moon Sign Scorpio*

am . . . .

pm . . . .
Today works best if you have enough time to do almost anything that takes your fancy. You can afford to put the usual responsibilities of everyday life on hold and capitalise on a frenzy of exciting possibilities. Following the dictates of those who don't know you at all well will probably not appeal to you now.

	LOVE	MONEY	CAREER	VITALITY

11 MONDAY ☿ *Moon Age Day 16 Moon Sign Sagittarius*

am . . . .

pm . . . .
You have scope to use a little cheek today and also to bring your personality to bear on practical matters. Prepare to capitalise on the chance to make progress at work, and to use the most appealing side of your nature to attract others. In other words, look out for possible advancement and get yourself noticed more!

12 TUESDAY ☿ *Moon Age Day 17 Moon Sign Sagittarius*

am . . . .

pm . . . .
Trends support a strong desire for personal freedom that is not easily thwarted. Be prepared to let it show at all times and under all circumstances, since you might feel very restricted if people or situations hold you back. Don't be afraid to stand up for the rights of others if you feel they are somehow getting short-changed or put upon.

13 WEDNESDAY ☿ *Moon Age Day 18 Moon Sign Capricorn*

am . . . .

pm . . . .
Your co-operative spirit is now enhanced, assisting you to make best use of your easy-going and affable nature. In any group-based encounters there are gains available if you give of your best and show just how reasonable you are capable of being. Even if other people are more dominant than you are, few will have your natural poise and charm.

14 THURSDAY ☿ *Moon Age Day 19 Moon Sign Capricorn*

am . . . .

pm . . . .
You could be quite unusually motivated now and can benefit from the fact that your intuitive powers are extremely well tuned. Today is about getting the best from others, and using this skill to achieve success at work and then later in social settings. This probably won't be an evening to stay in if you have the option to do something different.

15 FRIDAY   ☿   *Moon Age Day 20   Moon Sign Capricorn*

am . . . .

pm . . . .
You could now find that getting ahead with plans is not very easy. Trends suggest there may be complications to be dealt with, and not everyone might be as willing to compromise as you. Your best approach is to look out for pitfalls and for situations in which it would plainly be better to wait for another day than to be over-committed and fraught.

16 SATURDAY   ☿   *Moon Age Day 21   Moon Sign Aquarius*

am . . . .

pm . . . .
Mars is now in your solar second house, bringing a trend that does little to assist you in financial matters. Planning ahead could become somewhat more difficult, and you may decide to rethink your strategies with regard to something you wanted to buy for your home. If you are wise now, there are gains to be made later.

17 SUNDAY   ☿   *Moon Age Day 22   Moon Sign Aquarius*

am . . . .

pm . . . .
There are potential conflicts at work within your solar chart because although Mars is indicating certain problems with regard to cash, Venus assists you to iron them out. The result is that you may not know exactly where you are, and you could find alternating trends in action. Even if this is confusing, you also have scope to be entertained by it.

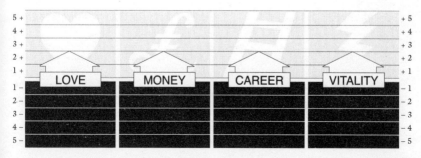

18 MONDAY ☿ *Moon Age Day 23   Moon Sign Pisces*

am . . . .

pm . . . .

New personal horizons are set by the arrival of the lunar high and your potential for success is increased. Even if things haven't been going badly, for today and tomorrow especially you can capitalise on an upward turn in your fortunes. There's nothing wrong with asking others to give you hand if you think it necessary.

19 TUESDAY ☿ *Moon Age Day 24   Moon Sign Pisces*

am . . . .

pm . . . .

They say that faith can move mountains, and this certainly seems to be the case for you right now. The lunar high offers greater hope and the possibility of achieving something you could have seen as being virtually impossible only a few days ago. This is the best time of the month to think about commencing something new.

20 WEDNESDAY ☿ *Moon Age Day 25   Moon Sign Aries*

am . . . .

pm . . . .

A communicative role of one sort or another is now indicated, and the more you keep in touch with the world at large, the greater are the rewards that you can achieve. You can best avoid unnecessary stresses and strains by getting other people to help you. This relates as much to things that pressure your mind as to any part of your body.

21 THURSDAY ☿ *Moon Age Day 26   Moon Sign Aries*

am . . . .

pm . . . .

The emphasis at the moment is on your natural curiosity. You might be particularly inquisitive today, and can use this to find out what makes things tick. Although this is a generally favourable trend, it might also encourage you to tinker more than would normally be the case. That's fine, just as long as you have some idea what you are doing!

22 FRIDAY *Moon Age Day 27   Moon Sign Aries*

am . . . .

pm . . . .
There is a strong sense of togetherness now, especially in terms of personal attachments. You have scope to be more romantically inclined than ever, and should be able to up the pace when it comes to relationships of almost any sort. Remember that if people find you attractive and approachable, they are more likely to seek your good offices.

23 SATURDAY *Moon Age Day 28   Moon Sign Taurus*

am . . . .

pm . . . .
Communication skills remain well accented, and it might be suggested that May is the month of the talker as far as Pisces is concerned. It's time to talk to loved ones, to colleagues and friends and also to absolute strangers, and you have what it takes to get a favourable response. If there is something you want, ask – because you could get it.

24 SUNDAY ☿ *Moon Age Day 0   Moon Sign Taurus*

am . . . .

pm . . . .
There are good reasons now to protect yourself emotionally – or that's the way it looks. Pisces does get hurt occasionally and that can make you wary about committing yourself. Actually you may well be in a stronger position all round than you think, and though it is natural for you to overreact it probably isn't necessary at present.

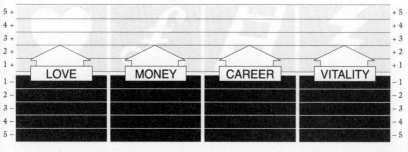

25 MONDAY ☿ *Moon Age Day 1 Moon Sign Gemini*

am . . . .

pm . . . .
A strong emphasis on work and productivity makes this an ideal time to work toward some kind of advancement. Some Pisces individuals may be thinking about a total change of job, and it's worth making the most of opportunities that would make such a change easier. Whatever you decide to do, be prepared to shine and let everyone else notice.

26 TUESDAY ☿ *Moon Age Day 2 Moon Sign Gemini*

am . . . .

pm . . . .
There might seem to be many reasons today why you can't let go completely and have a good time, yet when you start to look at life closely there might actually be no reason at all. It's natural to be wary, especially if you are a Pisces subject, but there are also days when it is fine to throw caution to the wind. That way, you can be truly alive.

27 WEDNESDAY ☿ *Moon Age Day 3 Moon Sign Cancer*

am . . . .

pm . . . .
You can afford to relax and pamper yourself today. The time is right to take things just a little slower, so that you can at least look to your own needs more than you generally do. It's also possible to persuade others to lend a hand if you ask them to do so. But do you feel it's sometimes easier and quicker to wade in and do things yourself?

28 THURSDAY ☿ *Moon Age Day 4 Moon Sign Cancer*

am . . . .

pm . . . .
Trends indicated that you may be going through one of your idealistic phases. That's fine, because if it weren't for Pisces, who would look after the world and nurture it? The only slight problem is if you are tempted to try to do too much. Also, it's important to ask yourself whether your efforts are truly as helpful as they might at first seem.

29 FRIDAY ☿ *Moon Age Day 5 Moon Sign Leo*

am . . . .

pm . . . .
The emphasis now is on the tedious things that need to be done, and on the effort that is necessary to complete them. At the same time there are planets around that assist you to delegate, and there is certainly no reason to worry about getting everything done yourself if there are other people around who you could coax into helping.

30 SATURDAY ☿ *Moon Age Day 6 Moon Sign Leo*

am . . . .

pm . . . .
Beware of taking on more than you can justifiably handle today. Trends highlight a tendency for you to want to get everything done at the same time. You also need to consider whether you are doing certain things out of a sense of habit. Perhaps it's time to reassess the very reason why you do some of the tasks you do, and to re-plan your strategy once and for all.

31 SUNDAY ☿ *Moon Age Day 7 Moon Sign Virgo*

am . . . .

pm . . . .
You would be wise to exercise a little caution in terms of money whilst the lunar low is around. It isn't necessarily that you are suddenly poorer, though there could be a tendency to throw good money after bad regarding an issue that might be best abandoned now. Why not seek support – and affection – from friends?

	LOVE	MONEY	CAREER	VITALITY

June 2009

YOUR MONTH AT A GLANCE

$\oplus$ = Opportunities are around $\ominus$ = Be on the defensive   = Life is pretty ordinary

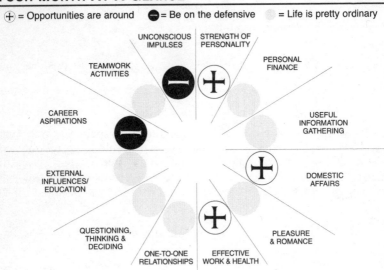

JUNE HIGHS AND LOWS

Here I show you how the rhythms of the Moon will affect you this month. Like the tide, your energies and abilities will rise and fall with its pattern. When it is above the centre line, go for it, when it is below, you should be resting.

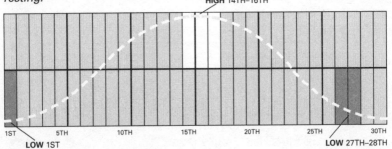

90

1 MONDAY
Moon Age Day 8   Moon Sign Virgo

am . . . .

pm . . . .
Progress may be slow, but despite the lunar low, it can be achieved. Your best approach is to do one thing at once and make certain you realise your objectives before moving on. It's worth applying your skills to sort out any agitation, particularly in relation to family matters. All in all you can make today better than expected.

2 TUESDAY
Moon Age Day 9   Moon Sign Libra

am . . . .

pm . . . .
Be prepared to curb any tendency at the moment to speak first and think later. If you are too quick in your reactions, you could bring unintended offence and then you will have to eat humble pie later. There are gains to be made through bringing new personalities into your life, and through being motivated to make major alterations at work.

3 WEDNESDAY
Moon Age Day 10   Moon Sign Libra

am . . . .

pm . . . .
The time is right to eliminate anything from your life that has run its course. If you take up this challenge you will be quite busy for most of the time, and could end up with a more streamlined way of living. It might be late for spring-cleaning but that doesn't mean it's irrelevant. It's still important to capitalise on what new people bring to your life.

4 THURSDAY
Moon Age Day 11   Moon Sign Scorpio

am . . . .

pm . . . .
There are good reasons to talk things through with those close to you. When something troubles you, there may well be people around who have just the right answer to help you, but they are not psychic and will need to be approached first. Family gatherings and social outings have much to offer you today.

5 FRIDAY
Moon Age Day 12   Moon Sign Scorpio

am . . . .

pm . . . .
Your inquiring mind can be turned up to full strength again, allowing you to turn over stones wherever you go, just to see what might lie beneath them. Even if some of the answers you come up with surprise you, your efforts should be worthwhile. One particularly good idea could form an important part of your long-term future.

6 SATURDAY
Moon Age Day 13   Moon Sign Scorpio

am . . . .

pm . . . .
This is a potentially hard-working phase during which you have scope to find plenty to keep you occupied. Now is the time to move closer and closer to achieving a longed-for objective and to be willing to see things in a very optimistic way. Seeking advice should be a natural aspect of life now, as should achieving plenty of variety across the weekend.

7 SUNDAY
Moon Age Day 14   Moon Sign Sagittarius

am . . . .

pm . . . .
Even if others disagree with some of your sentiments at this time, it's worth taking a reasonable approach in order to avoid falling out with anyone. Of course you could simply ignore what is being said and carry on in your own sweet way, but trends also support an urge within you to let people know the way you really feel now.

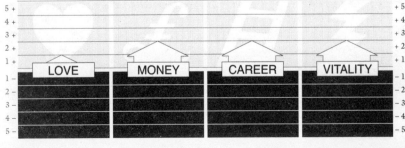

8 MONDAY *Moon Age Day 15   Moon Sign Sagittarius*

am . . . .

pm . . . .
Your overall outlook today inclines towards an easy-going composure
and an ability to deal with situations as and when they arise. If you are
looking for a peaceful sort of day, that is what you should find in the
main. You have what it takes to persuade people to accept your ideas and
proposals, particularly if you are positive in the way you put them across.

9 TUESDAY *Moon Age Day 16   Moon Sign Capricorn*

am . . . .

pm . . . .
It's time to capitalise on some surprising and maybe delightful
encounters with new people. When it comes to relationships, you would
be wise to expect the unexpected, and there are gains to be made from
the fact that life is offering you new challenges and opportunities. Casual
associates could prove to be quite useful to you in one way or another.

10 WEDNESDAY *Moon Age Day 17   Moon Sign Capricorn*

am . . . .

pm . . . .
Today could be favourable for journeys down memory lane. Pisces is
inclined to be quite nostalgic now and again, and can take great delight
in remembering people and places. However, this needn't get in the way
as far as your forward progress is concerned, especially if you are
determined to remain basically committed to a modern approach.

11 THURSDAY *Moon Age Day 18   Moon Sign Capricorn*

am . . . .

pm . . . .
Trends encourage you to be somewhat impulsive and very direct in the
way you deal with others today. That's fine, just as long as you pull your
punches a little in the case of people who are timid or worrying about
something. Your intuition is the best guide here, because very little goes
over your head. It's worth seeking warmth and support from friends.

12 FRIDAY
Moon Age Day 19   Moon Sign Aquarius

am . . . .

pm . . . .
Venus is now strong in your solar third house and this is an influence that favours travel of one form or another. Whether it's for business or pleasure, you can get a great deal out of moving about around at this time, and it doesn't matter if the journey is long or short. New advantages are there for the taking thanks to the solid effort you are putting in.

13 SATURDAY
Moon Age Day 20   Moon Sign Aquarius

am . . . .

pm . . . .
Today coincides with a good deal of confusion for some Pisces subjects. It may not be you who fails to understand what is required, but rather colleagues or friends. However, it could be up to you to sort things out, and that's where the fun might begin! New starts at work may be better than trying to revive tired plans from the past.

14 SUNDAY
Moon Age Day 21   Moon Sign Pisces

am . . . .

pm . . . .
Your level of self-belief is enhanced as the lunar high arrives, and you have what it takes to be on form in social situations and at work. You can get a great deal done and should easily be able to apply yourself to any task that seems necessary. Capitalise on the fact that Lady Luck is on your side and that she shines on you when you least expect it.

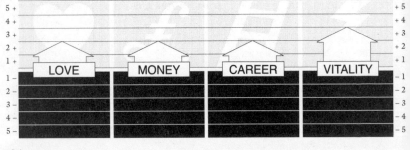

15 MONDAY
Moon Age Day 22   Moon Sign Pisces

am . . . .

pm . . . .

You can now tap into a higher level of physical vitality, allowing you to undertake a great deal of activity throughout the day. You could easily get bored if you are forced to remain in the same place for long at a time, and there is much to be said for getting as much change and diversity into your life as proves to be possible at the moment.

16 TUESDAY
Moon Age Day 23   Moon Sign Pisces

am . . . .

pm . . . .

For the third day in a row the lunar high helps you to make life easy-going and generally carefree. Today works best if you remain in a positive frame of mind and refuse to rise to any bait that others are offering. Arguments should be avoided like the plague, so that even when you are seriously provoked you are in a position simply to smile and walk away.

17 WEDNESDAY
Moon Age Day 24   Moon Sign Aries

am . . . .

pm . . . .

The time is right to create a pleasant atmosphere at home and to take great delight in good company. What might also please you at the present time is if you realise that others have put themselves out on your behalf. Acting on impulse would be no bad thing in social situations, and don't be surprised if you find amusement in family settings.

18 THURSDAY
Moon Age Day 25   Moon Sign Aries

am . . . .

pm . . . .

Even the most casual conversations have potential to inspire you with new confidence and give you excellent ideas for the future. Be sure to spend some time at the moment thinking about your own needs and wants. This isn't being selfish, particularly if you make sure that everything that comes good for you is turned into the favours you bring to others.

19 FRIDAY
Moon Age Day 26   Moon Sign Tauru

am . . . .

pm . . . .
There are gains to be made if you keep your overall attitude fairly tough
today. You needn't stand any nonsense from yourself or from others, and
although you can still be tactful, you will expect things to be done as and
when you say the time is right. The odd fall-out is possible at home
especially if people think you are lording it over them.

20 SATURDAY
Moon Age Day 27   Moon Sign Tauru

am . . . .

pm . . . .
The Moon in your solar third house supports a little mental restlessnes
and a feeling that you should perhaps be anywhere else than where you
happen to be at any particular point in time. Even if you are working to
the best of your ability, there's always a possibility that some of the job
you undertake will have to be done again later.

21 SUNDAY
Moon Age Day 28   Moon Sign Gemin

am . . . .

pm . . . .
There should be much to keep you assured and happy at home, thoug
you may also decide that it would be good to get away from your own
environment and out into the wider world. Any place that is beautiful o
that gives you food for thought would be ideal, and there is much to be
said for being in the company of people who stimulate your mind.

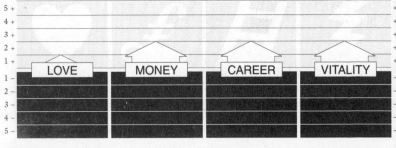

22 MONDAY
Moon Age Day 29   Moon Sign Gemini

am . . . .

pm . . . .
You now have scope to be very expressive when it comes to putting across your feelings. You can capitalise on favourable romantic trends by remaining warm in all your personal attachments. By the end of today you should be more aware than ever why you hold fast to the people who are so important to your life.

23 TUESDAY
Moon Age Day 0   Moon Sign Cancer

am . . . .

pm . . . .
The spotlight is on your ego at this time, and that could make you slightly difficult to deal with. Not that this need be too much of a problem, particularly if you are such a pleasant person to have around most of the time that people are willing to make allowances. Make the most of any new excitement that is happening at home.

24 WEDNESDAY
Moon Age Day 1   Moon Sign Cancer

am . . . .

pm . . . .
Tension is possible in discussions if you fail to take into account the fact that other people can have a very different view of life to the one you hold. One option is to avoid deep discussions altogether if you sense that all is not going well. Keeping your associations with others light and brief is the order of the day today.

25 THURSDAY
Moon Age Day 2   Moon Sign Leo

am . . . .

pm . . . .
You now have scope to sort out the most practical issues of the day, and to use your powers of thought to concentrate on serious issues when you have the time. Be prepared to respond to any sense of urgency that attends something that needs doing or around your home, and to offer support to your neighbours if required.

26 FRIDAY

Moon Age Day 3   Moon Sign Leo

am . . . .

pm . . . .
You have potential to be extremely creative and quite artistic under present astrological trends and will need to find outlets for this side of your nature. In a social or romantic sense you can be great company, and people should be pleased to have you around. Do you have time to respond to all the attention you are able to attract now?

27 SATURDAY

Moon Age Day 4   Moon Sign Virgo

am . . . .

pm . . . .
The lunar low comes along just as the weekend gets started. This need not be too much of a problem just as long as you realise that it won't be possible to do a thousand different things today. Your best approach is to pick what seems most important and make sure it is something that carries a strong sense of satisfaction. One job at once is essential.

28 SUNDAY

Moon Age Day 5   Moon Sign Virgo

am . . . .

pm . . . .
Even if you don't seem to have much influence regarding your life as a whole today, this may not be the case at all. On the contrary, every little thing you do makes a difference in the end – it's simply that you can't see far enough ahead. You can afford to take pleasure in the company of relatives, close friends, and of course your partner.

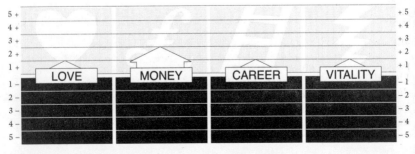

29 MONDAY

Moon Age Day 6   Moon Sign Libra

am . . . .

pm . . . .
Beware of getting yourself involved in any discussions that could turn
into arguments today. Mars is in your solar third house and that
encourages you to be more reactive in a verbal sense – and also probably
less tactful than would often be the case. Misunderstandings will be
possible, and sorting them out quickly is a top priority.

30 TUESDAY

Moon Age Day 7   Moon Sign Libra

am . . . .

pm . . . .
An ideal time to seek enjoyment and to appreciate your own best
qualities, which is not universally the case for Pisces. At this stage of the
week you will find that the more you put into life, the greater will be the
immediate rewards that you can achieve. Be prepared to respond to the
very special need that people have of you today.

1 WEDNESDAY

Moon Age Day 8   Moon Sign Libra

am . . . .

pm . . . .
That rather difficult position of Mars in your solar chart indicates the
possibility of a sarcastic and domineering Pisces today. This would not be
a positive situation, and might be all the more noticeable because this is
not the sort of individual you usually are. Make the first day of July
happier by eating a little humble pie. It doesn't taste so bad!

2 THURSDAY

Moon Age Day 9   Moon Sign Scorpio

am . . . .

pm . . . .
Useful and practical knowledge can be gained from a number of different
directions. In particular you have a chance to draw a great deal of
inspiration and plenty of assistance from your best friends. It might be
necessary to call upon professional expertise around now, especially
concerning equipment in and around your home.

3 FRIDAY

Moon Age Day 10   Moon Sign Scorpio

am . . . .

pm . . . .
Life can offer significant distractions at the moment, though many of
these will be available once the working day is over and you are in a
position to do what you wish. It might be all too easy at present to feel
fettered by responsibilities, and you would be wise to break out of
routines if at all possible. Work towards creating a happy end to the day.

4 SATURDAY

Moon Age Day 11   Moon Sign Sagittarius

am . . . .

pm . . . .
Be prepared to gain the support of authority figures, especially if you
need any special sort of help or advice around now. The warmth and
affection of friends can make all the difference at present, and socialising
is the name of the game this weekend. It doesn't matter how tired you
are, doing something different should wake you up quickly.

5 SUNDAY

Moon Age Day 12   Moon Sign Sagittarius

am . . . .

pm . . . .
Even if your practical common sense and your level of concentration are
not as noteworthy as would sometimes be the case, you might be quite
opinionated today and more than willing to offer your point of view.
Maybe you should do more listening than talking whilst Mars is in your
solar third house. Local issues are highlighted now.

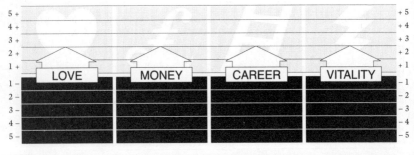

YOUR MONTH AT A GLANCE

$\oplus$ = Opportunities are around $\ominus$ = Be on the defensive   = Life is pretty ordinary

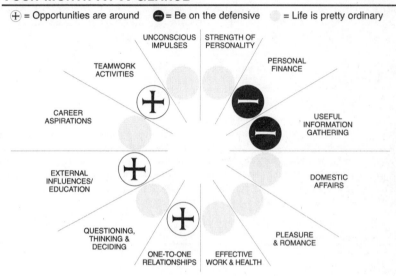

JULY HIGHS AND LOWS

Here I show you how the rhythms of the Moon will affect you this month. Like the tide, your energies and abilities will rise and fall with its pattern. When it is above the centre line, go for it, when it is below, you should be resting.

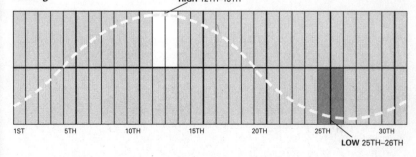

6 MONDAY   *Moon Age Day 13   Moon Sign Sagittarius*

am . . . .

pm . . . .
Being popular today should not involve a great deal of effort. On the contrary, you have what it takes to get people to respond to you from the moment you get out of bed. Don't try to go it alone today because you will get on much better if you rely on others. There are financial gains to be made and your general level of good luck is enhanced.

7 TUESDAY   *Moon Age Day 14   Moon Sign Capricorn*

am . . . .

pm . . . .
At home you can benefit from communication, and trends support a feeling now that you can get more or less all you want by saying the right thing. In the main this should work, but could be slightly less effective when you are dealing with colleagues or acquaintances. That is why you may decide to stick mostly to people you know well.

8 WEDNESDAY   *Moon Age Day 15   Moon Sign Capricorn*

am . . . .

pm . . . .
There is a chance of making new friends today and the opportunity to persuade even those who are generally difficult to deal with to be more compliant. This has potential to be a generally successful day and one that offers you a great deal more in the way of self-choice. Success is there for the taking in sporting activities or other competitive situations.

9 THURSDAY   *Moon Age Day 16   Moon Sign Aquarius*

am . . . .

pm . . . .
The focus is on your wish to feel wanted and, typical of your sign, you may be doing everything you can to be popular. Despite your best efforts there will always be some people around who won't work for your best interests, and it is important to be aware of the fact. There are some situations that demand a more direct approach on your part.

10 FRIDAY
Moon Age Day 17   Moon Sign Aquarius

am . . . .

pm . . . .
You have what it takes to be mentally keen today, but might also be quite opinionated. This may not go down well with everyone, and there are times when you need to relax more and to accept another point of view. Such a realisation won't come easy under present planetary trends. Prepare to respond to the demands of family members.

11 SATURDAY
Moon Age Day 18   Moon Sign Aquarius

am . . . .

pm . . . .
A quieter day is possible, mainly because the Moon is in your solar twelfth house. There are busier times on offer ahead, so there's nothing wrong with taking a rest today. That doesn't necessarily mean you will be doing nothing. On the contrary, the emphasis is on your social life, and on your desire to move around a good deal.

12 SUNDAY
Moon Age Day 19   Moon Sign Pisces

am . . . .

pm . . . .
The lunar high offers you greater levels of energy and a desire to ring the changes in a dozen different ways. Whether you will achieve everything you want today is another matter, but if you get halfway towards your objectives you will be doing well. Romance should be high on the agenda for Pisces now.

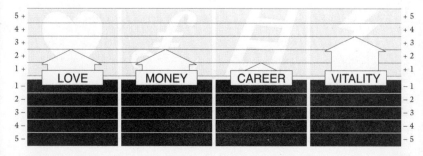

13 MONDAY
Moon Age Day 20   Moon Sign Pisces

am . . . .

pm . . . .

This is another day for pressing ahead with great confidence. This would be a favourable time to get onside with people who are successful and to learn from their attitudes and methods of working. There are gains to be made from examining your financial situation as it stands, plus the possibility of attracting more money in the near future.

14 TUESDAY
Moon Age Day 21   Moon Sign Aries

am . . . .

pm . . . .

Why not focus on having fun today? You have what it takes to get others to join in, and you can use the experience to broaden your horizons as much as possible. Some Pisces people will have chosen this time for a vacation, and if you are one of them, stand by to make it a holiday to remember!

15 WEDNESDAY
Moon Age Day 22   Moon Sign Aries

am . . . .

pm . . . .

You could resent being lumbered with obligations now, and in any dealings with others you need to be careful that you don't give any offence without realising that this is the case. A day to analyse your actions somewhat more carefully than you normally would and to talk things through, especially with close friends or your partner.

16 THURSDAY
Moon Age Day 23   Moon Sign Taurus

am . . . .

pm . . . .

There is confidence and assertiveness available in great measure. On occasions you might be slightly too confident for your own good, and a slightly more reserved approach sometimes suits you better. Temperamentally you are a natural co-operator and the fact needs to show at the moment if you are to make significant gains.

17 FRIDAY

Moon Age Day 24   Moon Sign Taurus

am . . . .

pm . . . .
A little discontent is possible now as the seesaw of life moves in the opposite direction. You are bound to have these ups and downs with so many mixed astrological trends about, but even on those occasions when things are not going entirely the way you would wish, you can still make a good deal of headway.

18 SATURDAY

Moon Age Day 25   Moon Sign Taurus

am . . . .

pm . . . .
Whatever is most meaningful to you at the moment can be gained via your family and the relationships that are most important to you. Your interests are best served this weekend by spending time in the company of people with whom you feel entirely at ease, and you may decide not to expand your social circle too much at present.

19 SUNDAY

Moon Age Day 26   Moon Sign Gemini

am . . . .

pm . . . .
You have the ability to really stand out in a crowd, though whether you will choose to do so today remains to be seen. What is probably true is that you will sparkle most on those occasions when you have little choice about being placed at the front of the class. Remember that being popular also means being available to give advice to others.

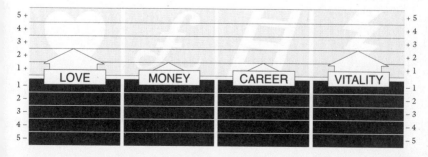

20 MONDAY   *Moon Age Day 27   Moon Sign Gemini*

am . . . .

pm . . . .
Circumstances assist you to put yourself firmly in the limelight this week, and that begins today. The sunny side of your personality can clearly be displayed, and you have what it takes to make everyone around you feel better. There could be more important abilities, but a great many people would swap their lives in order to be you.

21 TUESDAY   *Moon Age Day 28   Moon Sign Cancer*

am . . . .

pm . . . .
Enjoying your work is the order of the day at the moment, and you should be quite willing to take on new responsibilities whenever they are offered. Of course there is a limit, and you need to be careful not to push yourself so hard that something important gets forgotten. You might surprise yourself with your natural confidence today.

22 WEDNESDAY   *Moon Age Day 0   Moon Sign Cancer*

am . . . .

pm . . . .
This can be a positive phase of your life and a time during which you have scope to get a great deal done. The help you can obtain from others makes all the difference today, though there may be occasions when you need to push a little harder in order to get people to live up to their promises. Rules and regulations could very easily get on your nerves now.

23 THURSDAY   *Moon Age Day 1   Moon Sign Leo*

am . . . .

pm . . . .
Conditions at work can help you to propel yourself towards ever-greater achievements, and it looks as though you may have something that others really want. This puts you firmly in the driving seat and assists you to negotiate a good deal if it proves necessary. Hustling is not generally your thing, but you have the ability to do it now.

24 FRIDAY

Moon Age Day 2   Moon Sign Leo

am . . . .

pm . . . .
By tomorrow a potentially less helpful interlude arrives, but that is simply
the visit of the lunar low. You can use today to prepare yourself for the
weekend, perhaps by arranging something you can do that is easy on
your mind and not so demanding on your body either. A little relaxation
will do you no harm at all.

25 SATURDAY

Moon Age Day 3   Moon Sign Virgo

am . . . .

pm . . . .
How the weekend passes is entirely dependent on the way you approach
it. If you push yourself from morning until night, fatigue could be the
result, whereas if you take life in your stride and determine from the start
to have a good time, you have a chance to make it happen. Outside
circumstances might have little to do with your mood at present.

26 SUNDAY

Moon Age Day 4   Moon Sign Virgo

am . . . .

pm . . . .
The spotlight is on the opinions of other people today, and you may feel
as though you are the only one who isn't passionate about situations.
Bear in mind that the lunar low isn't the best time to get yourself into a
state about anything. Even if others run about like headless chickens, you
can afford to watch and wait in your quiet corner.

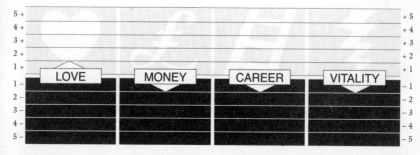

27 MONDAY
Moon Age Day 5   Moon Sign Libra

am . . . .

pm . . . .
You are now at your best when it comes to practical matters. The lunar low is out of the way and it's time to make full use of your common sense. You may still feel slightly lacking in overall vitality, but you needn't let that matter too much, particularly if you can persuade others that they should be doing things for you.

28 TUESDAY
Moon Age Day 6   Moon Sign Libra

am . . . .

pm . . . .
Personal matters and domestic trends are now well starred, and it is towards your home and family that you are encouraged to turn your mind at this stage. There are gains to be made through acting on impulse, though not so much that you enrage people with whom you are expected to co-operate. It is important to explain yourself fully.

29 WEDNESDAY
Moon Age Day 7   Moon Sign Scorpio

am . . . .

pm . . . .
This would be a very good time to organise family events or to get your relatives to do something that has been waiting in the wings for ages. Some might not want to co-operate, but you have very good persuasive skills at this time and will find it difficult to take no for an answer. You don't need to argue – simply turn on the charm!

30 THURSDAY
Moon Age Day 8   Moon Sign Scorpio

am . . . .

pm . . . .
It's time to take on new projects and capitalise on the slow but definite wind of change blowing around you at this time. There are gains to be made from new ideas that you can come up with, and from resurrecting a matter that began a long time ago. Much of what you planned in the past can now be played out on a more fortunate stage.

31 FRIDAY

Moon Age Day 9   Moon Sign Sagittarius

am . . . .

pm . . . .
Being around close friends is the name of the game today. Venus is now in your solar fourth house, which is also important when it comes to the love you feel for your nearest and dearest. Look carefully at your partner and work out how best you can really please them at the moment. Take them by surprise, and then watch the results unfold.

1 SATURDAY

Moon Age Day 10   Moon Sign Sagittarius

am . . . .

pm . . . .
Strong emotions emerge at the very beginning of August, and your best approach is to put all your natural warmth on display. This can help you to achieve popularity and to make the most of an opportunity to ask for something that you have wanted for ages. Who could resist you at the moment? You are so loveable you can get everyone on your side.

2 SUNDAY

Moon Age Day 11   Moon Sign Sagittarius

am . . . .

pm . . . .
Circumstances can be turned to your advantage for much of the time and you will be able to find just about everything you need at the moment. Of course there are always going to be disappointments, but if these occur at present they are probably of minor importance. Your best option is to find something else to capture your imagination.

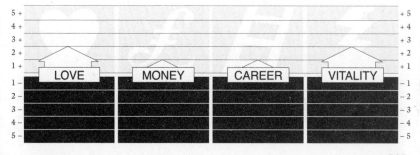

August 2009

YOUR MONTH AT A GLANCE

$\oplus$ = Opportunities are around ● = Be on the defensive ○ = Life is pretty ordinary

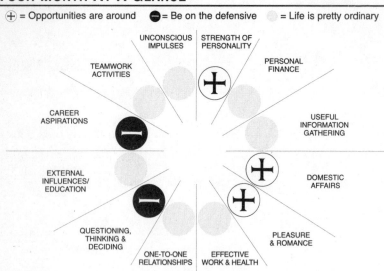

UNCONSCIOUS IMPULSES
STRENGTH OF PERSONALITY
TEAMWORK ACTIVITIES
PERSONAL FINANCE
CAREER ASPIRATIONS
USEFUL INFORMATION GATHERING
EXTERNAL INFLUENCES/ EDUCATION
DOMESTIC AFFAIRS
QUESTIONING, THINKING & DECIDING
PLEASURE & ROMANCE
ONE-TO-ONE RELATIONSHIPS
EFFECTIVE WORK & HEALTH

AUGUST HIGHS AND LOWS

Here I show you how the rhythms of the Moon will affect you this month. Like the tide, your energies and abilities will rise and fall with its pattern. When it is above the centre line, go for it, when it is below, you should be resting.

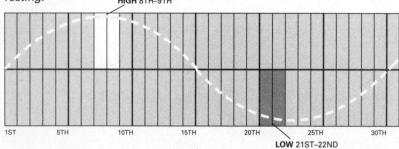

HIGH 8TH–9TH

LOW 21ST–22ND

1ST 5TH 10TH 15TH 20TH 25TH 30TH

3 MONDAY   *Moon Age Day 12   Moon Sign Capricorn*

am . . . .

pm . . . .
You have what it takes to get in someone's good books now and it is well
worth making the most of the fact. This is a great time for all matters
romantic and even for starting a new romance if you aren't attached
already. You might even discover that you have an admirer you never
suspected, because you are always the last one to realise.

4 TUESDAY   *Moon Age Day 13   Moon Sign Capricorn*

am . . . .

pm . . . .
New input you can elicit from others allows you to look at situations in
a brand new way. You should have more than you need in terms of
determination, and you can use your enhanced confidence to make some
real progress. It's amazing just how much difference it can make if people
see that you are raring to get going.

5 WEDNESDAY   *Moon Age Day 14   Moon Sign Aquarius*

am . . . .

pm . . . .
This may be the best time of the month for making vocational decisions
and even for thinking about a total change to your working life. A slightly
more reserved approach is indicated in your personal life, and you may
decide that this isn't the best time to speak your mind about romantic
issues. Be prepared to deal with inquisitive people today.

6 THURSDAY   *Moon Age Day 15   Moon Sign Aquarius*

am . . . .

pm . . . .
You can be at your most effective when it comes to work and the practical
dealings you have with the world at large. Where you might be less
successful is when it is necessary for you to be entirely truthful about your
own inner emotions. Pisces can often be a close book, partly because you
don't entirely understand yourself.

7 FRIDAY
Moon Age Day 16   Moon Sign Aquarius

am . . . .

pm . . . .

Another slightly quieter day, which is partly responsive to the position of the Moon in your solar twelfth house. This is something that always happens immediately ahead of the lunar high and it does at least offer you pause for thought before another period of quite significant activity. Rest in the shade and look out at the bright world beyond.

8 SATURDAY
Moon Age Day 17   Moon Sign Pisces

am . . . .

pm . . . .

You can make the most of this very progressive time and a period during which everything seems to sort itself out to your advantage. You may not have to interfere with things – simply allow them to unfold. This they will do quickly and in all manner of ways. You want to be entertained, but under the lunar high you can be the best act of all!

9 SUNDAY
Moon Age Day 18   Moon Sign Pisces

am . . . .

pm . . . .

This has potential to be a forward-moving phase during which you have what it takes to secure both the support and the friendships you crave. Do something different, even if it means changing your plans at the last moment, and get your friends to join in wherever possible. This can be the high point of August, and the possibilities are legion.

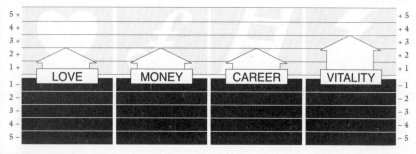

10 MONDAY
Moon Age Day 19   Moon Sign Aries

am . . . .

pm . . . .
Today is all about creating an interesting atmosphere in your social life, and the people you meet around now could well have a big part to play in your life later on. It's a fact that we all learn something new every day, and this is certain to be the case for Pisces subjects under present planetary trends.

11 TUESDAY
Moon Age Day 20   Moon Sign Aries

am . . . .

pm . . . .
Don't be surprised if you find that you are the subject of other people's warmth and affection. This could well be an indication of the good turns you have done previously, and the fact that people want to repay you for your kindness in the past. It isn't at all unusual for Pisces people to be held in the good esteem of others. It goes with the territory.

12 WEDNESDAY
Moon Age Day 21   Moon Sign Aries

am . . . .

pm . . . .
There are signs that some of the decisions you make today could seem unsound and might have little focus. You can't be on the ball all the time, and you may have to rely on the good offices and advice of friends in order to get what you want right now. In romantic attachments it's time to show how considerate you are capable of being.

13 THURSDAY
Moon Age Day 22   Moon Sign Taurus

am . . . .

pm . . . .
A day to bring some discipline and determination to the way you are acting, especially where work is concerned. Trying to accommodate the needs and wishes of everyone, especially relatives, might not be too easy now, but you have what it takes to find a way forward, just as long as you don't act too impulsively today or tomorrow.

14 FRIDAY   *Moon Age Day 23   Moon Sign Taurus*

am . . . .

pm . . . .
Trends encourage you to focus on both the past and your love of home and family at present, and you could be overtaken by waves of nostalgia and even longing for something that has gone. That's fine, but you must also remember that there is no future in the past, and that new opportunities lie around each corner.

15 SATURDAY   *Moon Age Day 24   Moon Sign Gemini*

am . . . .

pm . . . .
A slight touchiness is possible in your dealings with the world at large this weekend, and for this reason this is not an interlude that assists you in social situations. In many respects you might feel more comfortable at home, but even here there may be people who can easily rub you up the wrong way.

16 SUNDAY   *Moon Age Day 25   Moon Sign Gemini*

am . . . .

pm . . . .
Today is likely to be better when it comes to communicating with peers, associates and even casual acquaintances. The main spotlight is on your dealings with close friends, some of whom you might not get the chance to see too often. Make the most of small but important financial opportunities that are available to you today.

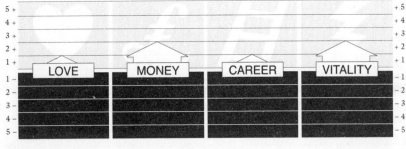

17 MONDAY
Moon Age Day 26   Moon Sign Cancer

am . . . .

pm . . . .
You now have scope to enjoy better, deeper and more meaningful romantic relationships. This is partly due to the present position of the Moon in your solar chart, but also responds to Venus. Be prepared to make the most of one of the most fortunate times of the summer when it comes to love, perhaps by committing yourself to a specific person.

18 TUESDAY
Moon Age Day 27   Moon Sign Cancer

am . . . .

pm . . . .
You can tap into plenty of energy around now and should be enjoying the best of what the summer has to offer, both socially and with regard to your urge to travel. Don't be forced to stay in once place all the time, at least not if you have any choice in the matter. You need change and diversity as well as new inspiration that travel offers.

19 WEDNESDAY
Moon Age Day 28   Moon Sign Leo

am . . . .

pm . . . .
It will be amazing just how much you can achieve today as a result of sheer discipline. Now is the time to show warmth and affection when it comes to your family, and loyalty when it comes to your friends. If you are determined to mix with new personalities all the time, it might be somewhat difficult to keep up with the social whirl!

20 THURSDAY
Moon Age Day 0   Moon Sign Leo

am . . . .

pm . . . .
Trends support a great need for fun and also the chance to enjoy some fairly unusual situations that come like a bolt from the blue. If the world and everyone in it seems particularly warm at the moment, this is probably a direct reflection of your own present attitudes. This should prove to you just how important our own actions and feelings really are.

21 FRIDAY

Moon Age Day 1   Moon Sign Virgo

am . . . .

pm . . . .
It may not be quite so easy to make the right decisions today, since the lunar low has the potential to cloud your judgement. There are so many positive planetary aspects and positions around now that you needn't let the lunar low have too much bearing on your life this month, though if things don't go your way it might be a different story!

22 SATURDAY

Moon Age Day 2   Moon Sign Virgo

am . . . .

pm . . . .
The danger of building on unsound foundations or else making decisions when you don't have all the information you need is definitely present. It is really important not to commit yourself to anything today unless you are absolutely certain of your facts. Leaving things for just one day shouldn't hurt, and will give you time to firm up your judgement.

23 SUNDAY

Moon Age Day 3   Moon Sign Libra

am . . . .

pm . . . .
Whether you like it or not, deferring to the choices other people are making may be a natural aspect of life around now. This is partly because the Sun has moved into your solar seventh house, which does nothing to enhance your own ability to plan your life. Take heart, because you have everything you need to get through slight problems and to triumph.

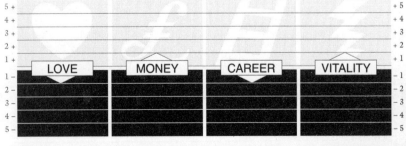

24 MONDAY
Moon Age Day 4   Moon Sign Libra

am . . . .

pm . . . .
In certain situations you might decide to take a more heavy-handed approach than has been the case recently, but this may be forced upon you by circumstances beyond your own control. Even if you feel that compromise is the best approach when dealing with relatives, at work you can afford to be rather more dominant, perhaps to the point of forcing issues.

25 TUESDAY
Moon Age Day 5   Moon Sign Scorpio

am . . . .

pm . . . .
This is a favourable time for any relationships that don't have any agendas attached to them. Complications come when you have too many things to bear in mind, so the more you can find situations that have flexibility built into them, the better you should feel. The focus is on making the most of a busy social scene, regardless of any setbacks.

26 WEDNESDAY
Moon Age Day 6   Moon Sign Scorpio

am . . . .

pm . . . .
Mercury has now entered your solar eighth house, encouraging a thirst for change and a desire to rid yourself of excess baggage that has been accumulating in your life. Bear in mind that this could be material objects you no longer use, or might represent feelings and emotions that are now only too clearly out of date.

27 THURSDAY
Moon Age Day 7   Moon Sign Scorpio

am . . . .

pm . . . .
A more rewarding period is on offer, and you need to capitalise on the present position of the Sun by ensuring you are in good company and also by showing just how inspirational and 'together' you can be. The social side of your nature is highlighted, and your ability to express yourself is now potentially better than for some days past.

28 FRIDAY
Moon Age Day 8   Moon Sign Sagittarius

am . . . .

pm . . . .
New colleagues can bring fresh perspectives at the very end of this week, and don't be surprised if one or two of them end up becoming friends as well. You show a good ability to mix business with pleasure ahead of the weekend and should be on top form when involved in any out-of-doors activity. Today is about just how good you look and feel.

29 SATURDAY
Moon Age Day 9   Moon Sign Sagittarius

am . . . .

pm . . . .
Your intuition is now firmly on target and you can afford to rely on those strong Piscean instincts. At the same time, taking yourself or anyone else too seriously isn't in your best interests, and there is much to be said for finding humour in situations. Beware of getting too involved in discussions that could easily turn into arguments.

30 SUNDAY
Moon Age Day 10   Moon Sign Capricorn

am . . . .

pm . . . .
You can elicit the good offices of almost anyone today – such is the natural charm you exude in almost all situations. Rather than struggling, it's worth seeking help from others, particularly people who really know what they are talking about. It's up to you to get on the right side of someone who has a particular skill that you need around now.

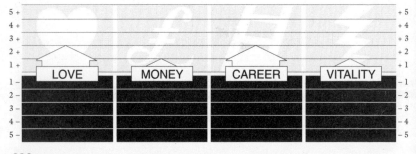

31 MONDAY
Moon Age Day 11   Moon Sign Capricorn

am . . . .

pm . . . .
It looks as though your talent for getting your message across can be as
strong this week as it has ever been. You can also make full use of an
uncanny knack of knowing how to adapt yourself in order to
accommodate the sensitivity of others. Try not to come over too strongly
when in the company of people who are naturally timid or shy.

1 TUESDAY
Moon Age Day 12   Moon Sign Capricorn

am . . . .

pm . . . .
As the first day of September progresses you encounter a twelfth-house
Moon, which supports a slightly more reflective interlude during which
you may be less inclined to push yourself forward in company. On the
contrary, there are good reasons to retreat into your shell, especially if it
seems your ideas are being questioned or your common sense examined.

2 WEDNESDAY
Moon Age Day 13   Moon Sign Aquarius

am . . . .

pm . . . .
This can be a time of personal growth, even if it might not seem that way
in a moment-by-moment sense today. Make sure the general direction of
your life is forward, and that you take every opportunity to work things
out to your satisfaction along the way. Unfortunately you will also be
slightly reserved now and not inclined to push issues at all.

3 THURSDAY
Moon Age Day 14   Moon Sign Aquarius

am . . . .

pm . . . .
Venus is now in your solar sixth house, offering you the chance to make
a change for the better in terms of your love life. Showing affection could
be the best way to gain a positive response from others, and even to
attract words of love you probably didn't expect. Don't be afraid to let
your natural affection spill over into the more practical side of your life.

4 FRIDAY

Moon Age Day 15   Moon Sign Pisces

am . . . .

pm . . . .

The lunar high offers enhanced energy, and you have what it takes to knock spots off any opposition. You shouldn't have to try all that hard to impress people, some of whom could be extremely important to you in the days and weeks ahead. Use any opportunity that comes your way to show just how capable you actually are.

5 SATURDAY

Moon Age Day 16   Moon Sign Pisces

am . . . .

pm . . . .

A stroke of luck could help you towards a chosen objective, and you appear to be able to fire on all cylinders in most situations. Don't take no for an answer once you have made up your mind about anything. Remember that you have the power to make any opposition you do come across today disappear like the morning mist.

6 SUNDAY

Moon Age Day 17   Moon Sign Pisces

am . . . .

pm . . . .

This continues to be a high-powered phase, but at the same time you should look for opportunities to enjoy whatever life has to offer outside of normal responsibilities. Why not spoil yourself a little if you get the chance today and allow others to make a fuss of you? Your ability to attract the natural affection of others is what really makes the difference now.

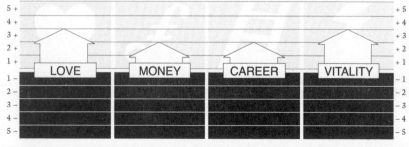

September 2009

YOUR MONTH AT A GLANCE

⊕ = Opportunities are around ⊖ = Be on the defensive ⬤ = Life is pretty ordinary

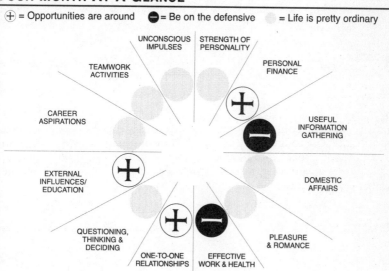

STRENGTH OF PERSONALITY

UNCONSCIOUS IMPULSES

TEAMWORK ACTIVITIES

PERSONAL FINANCE

CAREER ASPIRATIONS

USEFUL INFORMATION GATHERING

EXTERNAL INFLUENCES/ EDUCATION

DOMESTIC AFFAIRS

QUESTIONING, THINKING & DECIDING

ONE-TO-ONE RELATIONSHIPS

EFFECTIVE WORK & HEALTH

PLEASURE & ROMANCE

SEPTEMBER HIGHS AND LOWS

Here I show you how the rhythms of the Moon will affect you this month.
Like the tide, your energies and abilities will rise and fall with its pattern.
When it is above the centre line, go for it, when it is below, you should be
resting.

HIGH 4TH–6TH

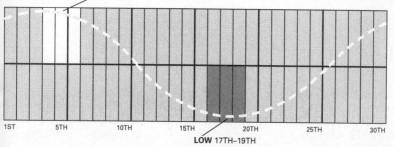

1ST   5TH   10TH   15TH   20TH   25TH   30TH

LOW 17TH–19TH

7 MONDAY ☿ *Moon Age Day 18   Moon Sign Aries*

am . . . .

pm . . . .
This is a great time to enjoy yourself. Don't be afraid to show the wider world what a larger-than-life character you can be, and make the most of this when you are in the company of like-minded people. Rather than getting hung up on details at work today, your best approach is to look at the bigger picture and enjoy the many diversions that you can discover.

8 TUESDAY ☿ *Moon Age Day 19   Moon Sign Aries*

am . . . .

pm . . . .
Plan to make the most of a boost in your powers of communication. As the day advances you should find it easier and easier to get others on your side and to make progress, even in directions that might have seemed somewhat difficult of late. You can attend to a variety of duties today and still have time left over to do what takes your fancy.

9 WEDNESDAY ☿ *Moon Age Day 20   Moon Sign Taurus*

am . . . .

pm . . . .
Trends encourage you to gravitate towards people who have influence and power. Being onside with those who are movers and shakers should make it easier for you to get what you want from life, especially in a professional sense. Today is also about enjoying yourself whilst you are working and making things happen throughout the whole day.

10 THURSDAY ☿ *Moon Age Day 21   Moon Sign Taurus*

am . . . .

pm . . . .
There are relationship trends around now which can be both pleasurable and supportive of your ego. The time is right to capitalise on the attention you can attract from others, and on the chance to express yourself fully. This is as true at home as out there in the wider world. Be prepared to address any issues that friends have at the moment.

11 FRIDAY
☿   *Moon Age Day 22*   *Moon Sign Gemini*

am . . . .

pm . . . .
Domestic matters come as an area of release from certain other pressures that might be surrounding you across the next couple of days. Your communication skills are still well accented, though it's possible that you are not being taken as seriously by some people as you would wish. For this reason you might decide that it's best to retreat a little.

12 SATURDAY
☿   *Moon Age Day 23*   *Moon Sign Gemini*

am . . . .

pm . . . .
Mars is now in your solar fifth house, so even if you feel that not everyone is taking you seriously, you may still be inclined to show off more than you normally would. There is much to be said for showing concern for things that are happening far from your own door, and your global conscience tends to be especially strong now.

13 SUNDAY
☿   *Moon Age Day 24*   *Moon Sign Cancer*

am . . . .

pm . . . .
Ask yourself whether it's time for a change, particularly if things seem to happen in the same old way time and again. This could relate to almost any sphere of your life, but is most likely to strike at home, perhaps when you are engaged in practical chores. Do what you can to alter your routines and where possible let the winds of change start to blow.

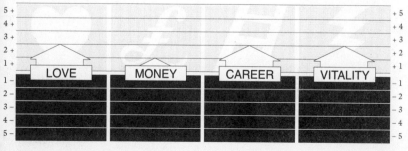

14 MONDAY ☿ *Moon Age Day 25   Moon Sign Cancer*

am . . . .

pm . . . .
You can now afford to feel easy-going and relaxed when you are around other people, and can use this interlude to make a particularly good impression on individuals who are in positions of authority. There might be a slight tendency for you to feel resentful if people don't come up to expectations, but have you really given them the chance?

15 TUESDAY ☿ *Moon Age Day 26   Moon Sign Leo*

am . . . .

pm . . . .
Right now the key to all work-related matters could involve attending to nagging details. This may not please you very much, because there are some planetary aspects around now that encourage you to look at the bigger picture. It's going to be a case of varying your methodology in order to suit prevailing circumstances.

16 WEDNESDAY ☿ *Moon Age Day 27   Moon Sign Leo*

am . . . .

pm . . . .
There is now a big emphasis on the romantic side of life and it is here that you can really make full use of the gregarious side of your nature. Beware though, because Mars is presently in your solar fifth house, and this can give you an ego the size of an elephant. Over-confidence and silly mistakes are a distinct possibility, so it's worth being on your guard.

17 THURSDAY ☿ *Moon Age Day 28   Moon Sign Virgo*

am . . . .

pm . . . .
As the lunar low comes along you might discover that something you thought was done and finished is rearing its head again. If extra work is necessary, a few frustrations might develop. Try to take things in your stride and tell yourself that not everything has to be completed at the same time. Think about which jobs can easily wait.

18 FRIDAY ☿ *Moon Age Day 29 Moon Sign Virgo*

am . . . .

pm . . . .
Don't be in the least surprised if certain things seem to be falling apart
today. However, you need to ask yourself whether this is actually the case.
Now is the time to stand back and look at things from a distance, and
consider your own attitude to the situation. You may decide to let others
do at least some of the work today while you have a rest.

19 SATURDAY ☿ *Moon Age Day 0 Moon Sign Virgo*

am . . . .

pm . . . .
If you use the influence of that very strong Mars to the best of your
ability today, you should see how useful it can actually be. You can create
an environment that is filled with confidence and certainty – all the more
so as the lunar low begins to fade from view. Romance could be on the
cards for Pisces subjects of varying ages.

20 SUNDAY ☿ *Moon Age Day 1 Moon Sign Libra*

am . . . .

pm . . . .
An ideal time to replace issues you have outgrown with new conditions
and possibilities. There is no point at all in hanging onto situations that
are doing you no good and which are nothing but a bother. However,
it's sometimes hard to see what these might be, and you need to be
entirely truthful with yourself at the moment.

	LOVE		MONEY		CAREER		VITALITY	

21 MONDAY ☿ *Moon Age Day 2   Moon Sign Libra*

am . . . .

pm . . . .
Prepare to bring a strong sense of movement into your life. Whenever it is obvious that you are standing still and doing nothing, your best approach is to engender some activity. With so much to gain you cannot afford to let the grass grow under your feet, especially at work. This week can offer new starts, a great sense of purpose and enterprising actions.

22 TUESDAY ☿ *Moon Age Day 3   Moon Sign Scorpio*

am . . . .

pm . . . .
You have scope to make relationships the big thing in your life during this part of the week. You should have as many people around you as proves to be possible because each individual has something different to tell you about life. Your strength now lies in your ability to learn lessons from the experiences of others.

23 WEDNESDAY ☿ *Moon Age Day 4   Moon Sign Scorpio*

am . . . .

pm . . . .
The Sun is now entering your solar eighth house and this brings a very important phase of the year. The eighth house is all about change and so across the next four weeks or so you are in a position to alter many situations – mostly in your favour. The story starts with you and a need to get rid of almost anything that is now redundant.

24 THURSDAY ☿ *Moon Age Day 5   Moon Sign Sagittarius*

am . . . .

pm . . . .
Career matters may bring only moderate advancement, if anything is actually changing at all. What might be necessary is a more decisive approach on your part, plus a definite knowledge of what you want and plans for how you intend to get it. If things don't line up on their own today, a greater input from you may be required.

25 FRIDAY   ☿   *Moon Age Day 6   Moon Sign Sagittarius*

am . . . .

pm . . . .
Venus is in your seventh house, which is favourable for relationships and
for all sorts of friendships and associations. Make the most of your magic
touch at the moment when you are dealing with other people, and enjoy
the popularity you can achieve. It would be extremely difficult to outstay
your welcome today.

26 SATURDAY   ☿   *Moon Age Day 7   Moon Sign Capricorn*

am . . . .

pm . . . .
Continual changes and transformations are the order of the day, assisting
you to keep yourself on the move. You may not take kindly at the
moment to having your wings clipped by anyone, and can afford to fight
strenuously to preserve your independence. If you feel stifled in any way
it is clear that the time is right to let people know how you really feel.

27 SUNDAY   ☿   *Moon Age Day 8   Moon Sign Capricorn*

am . . . .

pm . . . .
Even if you have made a good impression on the world at large, you could
still feel slightly frustrated if it seems that someone in particular is taking
little or no notice of you. Bear in mind that forcing yourself on others
probably won't work at all. There are gains to be made from finding a
middle path and also leaving time to pursue your own specific interests.

5 +				+ 5
4 +				+ 4
3 +				+ 3
2 +				+ 2
1 +				+ 1
1 −	LOVE	MONEY	CAREER	VITALITY	− 1
2 −				− 2
3 −				− 3
4 −				− 4
5 −				− 5

28 MONDAY ☿ *Moon Age Day 9   Moon Sign Capricorn*

am . . . .

pm . . . .

You can be rather impressionable at the moment and could be somewhat too sensitive to what you think other people are saying. As a rule you are very good at reading between the lines, but this might not be the case today. A little peace and quiet would be no bad thing later in the day, together with the opportunity to put your feet up.

29 TUESDAY ☿ *Moon Age Day 10   Moon Sign Aquarius*

am . . . .

pm . . . .

The time is right for an intense focus on your personal life. In many respects you would be wise to cut back on unnecessary activities and concentrate on what you know to be of supreme importance. In your association with the world at large you have a chance to show your great wisdom, and to use it to give advice and support to others.

30 WEDNESDAY ☿ *Moon Age Day 11   Moon Sign Aquarius*

am . . . .

pm . . . .

You now have potential to be at your most persuasive with others. Whatever it is that you want, you clearly have the ability to get it and you should be more than willing to go the extra mile in order to convince people of your sincerity. It doesn't matter whether you are teaching or learning, because in the end the two might turn out to be exactly the same!

1 THURSDAY *Moon Age Day 12   Moon Sign Pisces*

am . . . .

pm . . . .

Look for a definite window of opportunity as the lunar high arrives today and use it in order to get ahead of the crowd. Almost anyone you meet might turn out to be pivotal to your plans and therefore your future, so you have to keep paying attention. This could well be a very busy day, but one that could offer you far more than you have been expecting.

2 FRIDAY
Moon Age Day 13   Moon Sign Pisces

am . . . .

pm . . . .

The promising period continues, and today is one of those days during which you create your own good luck as you go along. New dreams and schemes are there for the taking, and these can help you to move closer to your heart's desire. In romantic situations you have all the golden words necessary to knock someone right off their feet.

3 SATURDAY
Moon Age Day 14   Moon Sign Pisces

am . . . .

pm . . . .

Do be ready to get rid of any dead wood that has been accumulating in your life recently. The path ahead of you seems quite clear, and you shouldn't be lacking when it comes to using initiative and even cunning. An ideal time to welcome people you don't see very often back into your life across the weekend, and to enjoy what they can bring.

4 SUNDAY
Moon Age Day 15   Moon Sign Aries

am . . . .

pm . . . .

Trends support a great urge on your part to get on well with others and to involve them more and more in your plans. Today is all about seeing well ahead of yourself in most situations and backing your intuition. Some people might even call you psychic at the moment, because it is so easy for you to assess how any particular situation will turn out.

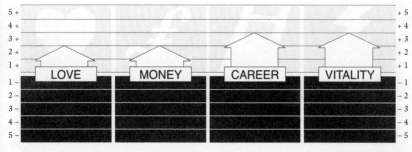

October 2009

YOUR MONTH AT A GLANCE

➕ = Opportunities are around   ➖ = Be on the defensive   ⬤ = Life is pretty ordinary

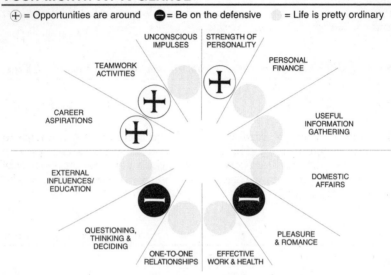

OCTOBER HIGHS AND LOWS

Here I show you how the rhythms of the Moon will affect you this month. Like the tide, your energies and abilities will rise and fall with its pattern. When it is above the centre line, go for it, when it is below, you should be resting.

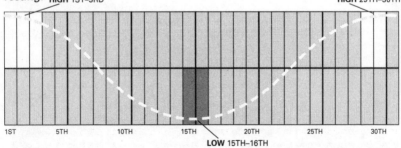

5 MONDAY
Moon Age Day 16   Moon Sign Aries

am . . . .

pm . . . .
You are a zodiac sign with a natural talent for communication at the moment. Mercury is in a really good position in your chart and it should help you to keep chatting on throughout the whole day and beyond. You might even talk in your sleep, so keen are you at the moment to let people know how you really feel about everything.

6 TUESDAY
Moon Age Day 17   Moon Sign Taurus

am . . . .

pm . . . .
The scope for personal freedom is strong and there are good rewards to be had from letting the world know that you are available and ready to take action. There may be occasions when you need to be rather forceful in the way you get your message across, and that could shock those who are used to your quiet ways.

7 WEDNESDAY
Moon Age Day 18   Moon Sign Taurus

am . . . .

pm . . . .
Keeping relationships harmonious is the name of the game, and you can afford to let romance colour your attitudes and your day right now. At this stage of the week your best approach is to watch and wait, and to remain willing to co-operate at work and to compromise if it proves to be necessary. Reap the benefits of allowing new personalities into your life.

8 THURSDAY
Moon Age Day 19   Moon Sign Gemini

am . . . .

pm . . . .
Change for the better is something you can now accomplish quite easily if you keep your mind clear and your attitudes sound and reasonable. Even if not everyone you deal with is quite as fair and open-minded as you are, the focus is on your ability to show just how patient you can be, which could prove to be very important.

9 FRIDAY

Moon Age Day 20   Moon Sign Gemini

am . . . .

pm . . . .
It's worth trying to glean important information from your partner or those to whom you are particularly close. Be prepared to keep your eyes and ears open because it is possible to help yourself at every stage of today. Make the most of opportunities to use your skills to clarify and resolve issues, particularly if others seem rather confused!

10 SATURDAY

Moon Age Day 21   Moon Sign Gemini

am . . . .

pm . . . .
Powerful ego tendencies now begin to show, and although these could cause you the odd problem, in the main they offer you scope to show how much you are enjoying life and how capable you actually are when it comes to getting things done. Even if not everyone wants to be your friend today, you can persuade those people you care about to adore you.

11 SUNDAY

Moon Age Day 22   Moon Sign Cancer

am . . . .

pm . . . .
This would be an ideal period to sort out certain aspects of your life and to make sure that what is going on around you is what you really need. This may not be universally the case and some adjustments could be necessary. Even if you turn this into a practical sort of Sunday, there ought to be room for enjoyment too, perhaps with your family.

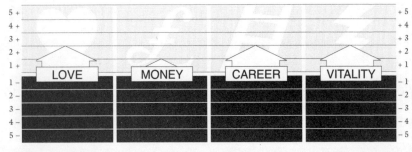

12 MONDAY
Moon Age Day 23   Moon Sign Cancer

am . . . .

pm . . . .
The spotlight is on bringing matters at work to a satisfactory conclusion
and on solving any problems that have been dogging you for a while.
There are many insights available to you around now, and a good deal of
coming and going may well be necessary in order to get all those
important details right.

13 TUESDAY
Moon Age Day 24   Moon Sign Leo

am . . . .

pm . . . .
You may now desire to change your personal lifestyle, but do you have
everything in place to make this possible? It is important to look at the
details and to make sure everything is organised in the way you want it
to be. Joint business matters are to the fore, and the thought of financial
gain can be very inspiring!

14 WEDNESDAY
Moon Age Day 25   Moon Sign Leo

am . . . .

pm . . . .
You would be wise to keep up your efforts for today and make sure that
all necessary jobs are done before tomorrow. The lunar low is on its way
and this time around it can offer a complete break and a retreat from
some of life's pressures. This is necessary on occasions so that you can
recharge your batteries and get the rest your body requires.

15 THURSDAY
Moon Age Day 26   Moon Sign Virgo

am . . . .

pm . . . .
You may decide there is no sense in trying too hard today because you
would simply be knocking your head against a brick wall. You can afford
to let others take the strain while you sit back and enjoy the show. Staying
close to home when it is possible to do so would be no bad thing, and
any new projects are probably best left until the weekend.

16 FRIDAY
Moon Age Day 27   Moon Sign Virgo

am . . . .

pm . . . .
For once your people skills may not be highlighted. This isn't like you at all, but your accustomed intuition is now less evident than usual, as is your patience. Even if this isn't the best end to the working week you have ever experienced, you should at least have kept your powder dry for later efforts. By the evening you can make sure things are looking better.

17 SATURDAY
Moon Age Day 28   Moon Sign Libra

am . . . .

pm . . . .
There is much to be said for breaking with some of your usual routines and trying out newer and more interesting possibilities. Just make sure that you don't throw out the baby with the bathwater. It might seem at first as if a certain ruthlessness is required, but if this really isn't your style, it may not work very well.

18 SUNDAY
Moon Age Day 0   Moon Sign Libra

am . . . .

pm . . . .
Once more you have scope to transform your personal life. This doesn't necessarily mean dumping relationships or insisting on changing everything for the sake of it. What is much more likely is that you are setting new trains in motion and then watching closely to see what happens. This evening brings strong social inclinations.

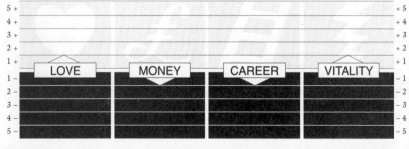

19 MONDAY
Moon Age Day 1   Moon Sign Scorpio

am . . . .

pm . . . .
You can now easily influence other people with your views and with the
way you are talking. An inspirational approach works best, and should be
appreciated by others. You need to be aware of any coincidences that
crop up today. Some of these can act as signposts to show you whether
your life is going in exactly the right direction.

20 TUESDAY
Moon Age Day 2   Moon Sign Scorpio

am . . . .

pm . . . .
Your need to analyse and to probe is highlighted more than ever, and that
famous Piscean curiosity is assisting you to put yourself in potentially
fortunate situations. Answering questions can now be your forte, and you
can put this skill to good use if colleagues and friends turn to you for
advice. What matters the most now is your originality.

21 WEDNESDAY
Moon Age Day 3   Moon Sign Sagittarius

am . . . .

pm . . . .
Now is the time to dispense with some of the usual formalities and cut
right to the chase. This can help you to achieve a generally successful day
and assist you to make gains you may not have even expected. Money
matters can be made more settled, and you have chances to make gains
from relatively unexpected directions.

22 THURSDAY
Moon Age Day 4   Moon Sign Sagittarius

am . . . .

pm . . . .
You generally have a good psychological understanding of your own
nature and those of the people with whom you interact. This is especially
true at the moment, and it allows you to second-guess the way they are
likely to react under any given circumstance. Your ability to solve
problems can make all the difference now.

23 FRIDAY   *Moon Age Day 5   Moon Sign Sagittarius*

am . . . .

pm . . . .
Create some opportunities today to understand those around you and to enjoy special times with your lover. For those Pisces subjects who are presently between relationships, there is much you can do to change the situation. A new love is definitely possible, but you need to ask yourself whether you are happier on your own at the moment.

24 SATURDAY   *Moon Age Day 6   Moon Sign Capricorn*

am . . . .

pm . . . .
You have what it takes to be both adventurous and optimistic across the weekend and to move the odd mountain if the desire to do so takes your fancy. There is also an emphasis on your level of physical motivation. Whatever you decide to take on today will work out best if you maintain your great determination.

25 SUNDAY   *Moon Age Day 7   Moon Sign Capricorn*

am . . . .

pm . . . .
Even if you feel slightly more impatient today, you needn't let that take the edge off your competitive instincts at all – in fact it could heighten them. By all means do whatever you can to obtain your objectives, though you could lose friends on the way if you are too ruthless. Such phases as this never last long for peaceful Pisces.

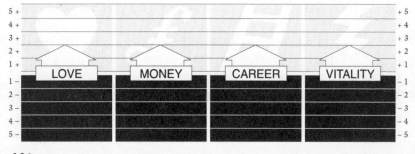

26 MONDAY
Moon Age Day 8   Moon Sign Aquarius

am . . . .

pm . . . .
You should be able to ensure that relationships are working out especially well at the beginning of this week. At the same time you are entering a slightly dreamy phase for the next couple of days, and it may be difficult to keep yourself motivated or physically inclined. Learn that a great deal can also be gained from meditating and waiting in the wings.

27 TUESDAY
Moon Age Day 9   Moon Sign Aquarius

am . . . .

pm . . . .
This is a time to allow wider interests to enter your life, even if you are looking at the possibilities in a slightly low-key way for the moment. There should be time to make up your mind and less pressure being placed upon you than was the case earlier in the month. All in all you can afford to feel quite good about yourself around now.

28 WEDNESDAY
Moon Age Day 10   Moon Sign Aquarius

am . . . .

pm . . . .
Today is about being gentle on yourself and also kind in the way you approach the world at large. Make sure this fact is not lost on other people. Although there will always be some folk around who take advantage of your good nature, in the main this will not be the case. Get onside with colleagues who have ambitious plans and show your support.

29 THURSDAY
Moon Age Day 11   Moon Sign Pisces

am . . . .

pm . . . .
The lunar high assists you to make the most of any career opportunities that are available. It is important to pay attention because many benefits today will come like a bolt from the blue. This is the time of the month when you have to realise that life is not a rehearsal and that what you get out of it is directly responsive to what you have first put in.

30 FRIDAY
Moon Age Day 12   Moon Sign Pisces

am . . . .

pm . . . .
You can rely on your personal charm to a great extent today and you should discover that Lady Luck has more than a small part to play in your fortunes. This is particularly the case if you can grab opportunities as they come along and remain wide-awake to all of them. A day to tap into the friendship and support of those around you.

31 SATURDAY
Moon Age Day 13   Moon Sign Aries

am . . . .

pm . . . .
This is the ideal time to reflect for a little while on what has happened during October and how you can best use any good fortune that has come your way in order to get on better later. There should also be time for a good heart-to-heart with your partner or a family member who needs your support. By all means give advice, but avoid taking over.

1 SUNDAY
Moon Age Day 14   Moon Sign Aries

am . . . .

pm . . . .
When it comes to the practical side of your nature the focus is on your good ideas and your knowledge of how to put them into practice. Rather than worrying about inconsequential details today, why not simply get on with doing what you know is correct? Even if others express doubts, you have what it takes to smile and carry on anyway.

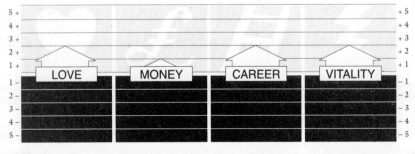

November
2009

YOUR MONTH AT A GLANCE

⊕ = Opportunities are around   ⊖ = Be on the defensive   ⬤ = Life is pretty ordinary

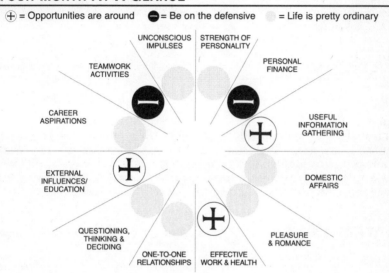

NOVEMBER HIGHS AND LOWS

Here I show you how the rhythms of the Moon will affect you this month. Like the tide, your energies and abilities will rise and fall with its pattern. When it is above the centre line, go for it, when it is below, you should be resting.

HIGH 25TH–27TH

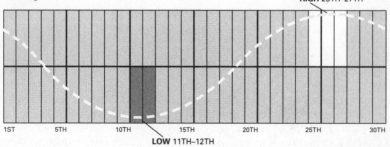

1ST   5TH   10TH   15TH   20TH   25TH   30TH

LOW 11TH–12TH

2 MONDAY
Moon Age Day 15   Moon Sign Aries

am . . . .

pm . . . .
Working on business projects could be interesting, though there are times today when you may decide you are happy to let others take the strain whilst you find newer and better ways to get things done. The fact is that you can be inspirational at present, and should be ready to show an unsuspecting world that you can achieve much when left to get on with it.

3 TUESDAY
Moon Age Day 16   Moon Sign Taurus

am . . . .

pm . . . .
In terms of your mental skills you should be sharp as a pin, and it would probably take someone extremely clever to pull the wool over your eyes at present. New ideas and breakthroughs are definitely possible, and you seem to be entering a phase that allows you to take control to a much greater extent. If you need support today, why not ask friends?

4 WEDNESDAY
Moon Age Day 17   Moon Sign Taurus

am . . . .

pm . . . .
Trends indicate that any plan of action might need addressing and maybe altering, even before you have really got started. Actually that is the time to make changes because once things really get going you will be too occupied. Pisces is rarely as go-getting as it is at present, so rather than standing around waiting, it's time to get stuck in!

5 THURSDAY
Moon Age Day 18   Moon Sign Gemini

am . . . .

pm . . . .
You should now be in a position to gain help in the form of very special relationships you enjoy with specific individuals, either at work or in a social sense. It's natural to turn to those who have been friends for a very long time and therefore people you know you can trust. However, even strangers have their part to play today or tomorrow.

6 FRIDAY
Moon Age Day 19   Moon Sign Gemini

am . . . .

pm . . . .
There is a strong emphasis on both social and romantic possibilities as the working week draws to its close. If you are looking for love, don't be afraid to consider methods you haven't tried before in order to get to meet the right person. The extreme warmth and kindness of all Pisces people should be apparent under present trends.

7 SATURDAY
Moon Age Day 20   Moon Sign Cancer

am . . . .

pm . . . .
Intellectual and philosophical interests are the order of the day for at least some of your time as the weekend gets started. At the same time you may well have itchy feet, and a shopping spree with friends would be no bad thing. Christmas isn't very far away, so the time is right to look for some real bargains. Spending wisely is the key at present.

8 SUNDAY
Moon Age Day 21   Moon Sign Cancer

am . . . .

pm . . . .
It might be all too easy today to get at cross-purposes with people you need to charm, particularly if you haven't checked on certain details or facts. The way you approach others is now extremely important because there are people around who can offer you so much. Today is much more about physicality than spirituality.

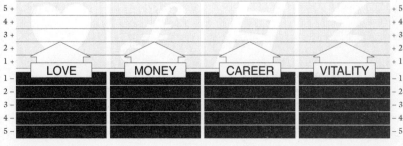

9 MONDAY
Moon Age Day 22   Moon Sign Leo

am . . . .

pm . . . .
In a social sense there may be a few ups and downs to deal with right
now. There is much to be said for getting out there and doing new
things. If circumstances hold you back or dictate that you are stuck in
one place all the time, a little frustration could follow. This is a week to
take charge of your own destiny if at all possible.

10 TUESDAY
Moon Age Day 23   Moon Sign Leo

am . . . .

pm . . . .
Now you need to find constructive outlets for the masses of energy that
you have at your disposal. Whilst other zodiac signs find difficulty with
the onset of the winter, you should be able to cope with it very well
indeed. At work this would be an ideal time to take a step up the ladder
of advancement, even if you have doubts about this.

11 WEDNESDAY
Moon Age Day 24   Moon Sign Virgo

am . . . .

pm . . . .
Don't be too surprised if circumstances seem to hold you back today. The
lunar low comes along, giving you no assistance in your efforts to do
what comes naturally. This is not to suggest that your own choices are
impossible, but extra effort will be required. Make full use of your
inquisitive mind and your desire to find out specific facts.

12 THURSDAY
Moon Age Day 25   Moon Sign Virgo

am . . . .

pm . . . .
Situations of one sort or another could well try your patience now, and
you may not have the level of tolerance for which your zodiac sign is
justifiably famous. On the plus side, there are good reasons to agitate for
things you consider are absolutely vital, and you needn't take no for an
answer when you are certain of your ground.

13 FRIDAY
Moon Age Day 26   Moon Sign Libra

am . . . .

pm . . . .
Capitalise on a more light-hearted trend that starts now the lunar low is out of the way. It might be increasingly hard for you to take anything very seriously and you need to take full advantage of the many new ideas that are available around now. Opportunities for long-distance travel are particularly well starred at the moment.

14 SATURDAY
Moon Age Day 27   Moon Sign Libra

am . . . .

pm . . . .
The way you approach your life in a general sense enables you to bring happiness to others, sometimes at the expense of your own desires. This is less likely to be true at present because you clearly have what it takes to make everyone else comfortable with their lives, whilst at the same time finding contentment yourself.

15 SUNDAY
Moon Age Day 28   Moon Sign Scorpio

am . . . .

pm . . . .
You need to find new input in order to make sure that some of your most cherished plans are not going to falter. It is important for you to feel that things generally are working out as you have intended, even if an extra push is necessary here and there. Why not use at least part of today to spend time proving your affection romantically?

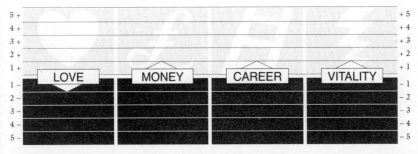

16 MONDAY
Moon Age Day 29   Moon Sign Scorpio

am . . . .

pm . . . .
By all means focus your energies on professional matters but learn to leave these alone once the working day is over. There is much more to your life than practical considerations and especially so under present planetary trends. New friendships are possible, together with an important realisation regarding someone you already know.

17 TUESDAY
Moon Age Day 0   Moon Sign Scorpio

am . . . .

pm . . . .
The focus is on travel whilst the Sun remains in your solar ninth house, perhaps to exotic or distant places. Trends also enhance your intellectual curiosity, encouraging you to persevere in order to get to the bottom of puzzles or issues. Even people can stimulate your mind, and it is suddenly very important to know their motivations.

18 WEDNESDAY
Moon Age Day 1   Moon Sign Sagittarius

am . . . .

pm . . . .
You can turn this into another favourable time as far as your career is concerned. If you know exactly how things ought to be going, you should be doing all you can to alter circumstances to suit your mental pattern. It shouldn't be hard to get others involved in your schemes, and it seems as if everyone wants to be on your team now.

19 THURSDAY
Moon Age Day 2   Moon Sign Sagittarius

am . . . .

pm . . . .
You can get the best from most situations simply by being what nature made you. Today is about putting your natural kindness on display, and you have what it takes to inspire colleagues and friends. Make the most of the popularity you are able to achieve, and the fact that your smiling face is dear to all sorts of individuals, some of whom you don't even count as being particular friends.

20 FRIDAY
Moon Age Day 3   Moon Sign Capricorn

am . . . .

pm . . . .
The Moon has now moved into your solar eleventh house, and for a day or two you might seem slightly more distant and difficult for others to understand. There's nothing wrong with retreating more into your own world, though it might be a journey that others simply cannot take. You should still be aware of how to complete practical demands.

21 SATURDAY
Moon Age Day 4   Moon Sign Capricorn

am . . . .

pm . . . .
You needn't let anything get in the way of your intellectual curiosity at this time, even if you express it in a slightly quieter way than you did a few days ago. If you really do need to know why situations are the way they are, this is an ideal time to turn over stones on the path of life, simply so you can find out what might be hiding beneath them.

22 SUNDAY
Moon Age Day 5   Moon Sign Capricorn

am . . . .

pm . . . .
The Moon in your solar twelfth house now offers a somewhat quieter interlude than usual, and friends might wonder if there is something bothering you. Even if this is not the case, you may well decide you don't have the same need for company as you usually do. One option is simply to remain alone today.

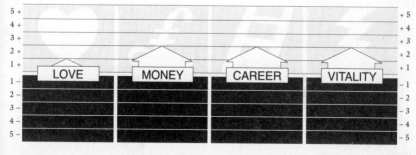

23 MONDAY

Moon Age Day 6   Moon Sign Aquarius

am . . . .

pm . . . .
You can afford to make work the single most important motivating factor for the moment, and to let your social life take a back seat until the middle of the week. Today works best if you only deal with one major situation at a time and are willing leave everything else alone. An inability to multi-task is the most evident result.

24 TUESDAY

Moon Age Day 7   Moon Sign Aquarius

am . . . .

pm . . . .
Meetings with others can help you expand your horizons no end, and you can slowly but surely come out of your shell as the Moon moves towards your zodiac sign of Pisces. Hour by hour you will be demonstrating your ability to think logically but also to bear in mind that tremendous Piscean intuition. Allow people to marvel at your insights.

25 WEDNESDAY

Moon Age Day 8   Moon Sign Pisces

am . . . .

pm . . . .
The lunar high can be especially fruitful this month and assists you to move closer than ever to getting something important working in your life. At the same time you have what it takes to inspire others to work on your behalf, which they should do quite naturally because of their affection for you. Finances can also be strengthened now.

26 THURSDAY

Moon Age Day 9   Moon Sign Pisces

am . . . .

pm . . . .
Prepare to pursue success and to get things going your way. This shouldn't simply be a case of better luck, because you have what it takes to put in so much extra effort that you deserve to succeed. You can even persuade those who have not been on your side in the recent past to understand your true motivations and to join forces with you.

27 FRIDAY
Moon Age Day 10   Moon Sign Pisces

am . . . .

pm . . . .
Trends assist you to make all the right moves, especially at work. If you are presently involved in full-time education you should be able to find out something to your advantage, and all Pisceans can take advantage of better financial prospects quite soon. Look out for a magnetic stranger who might have something to offer you.

28 SATURDAY
Moon Age Day 11   Moon Sign Aries

am . . . .

pm . . . .
By all means enjoy the successes you have achieved in different spheres of your life, though it has to be said that you may also be filled with burning desires that are not too easy to address or to achieve. It is so often the case that at the core of Pisces there is a divine discontent, often brought about because of slightly unrealistic expectations.

29 SUNDAY
Moon Age Day 12   Moon Sign Aries

am . . . .

pm . . . .
Freedom can be the key to happiness at present and there isn't much doubt that you will be at your best when you have hours in front of you to spend doing whatever takes your fancy. Not that you need to spend these alone. Your social motivation is strong, and you can use it to get yourself involved in joyful events.

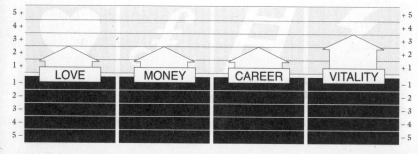

30 MONDAY
Moon Age Day 13   Moon Sign Taurus

am . . . .

pm . . . .
The focus is on your increased self-confidence and a desire to have things work out the way you expect. All the more reason to refuse to take no for an answer when it comes to social invitations you are handing out. Many Piscean individuals will already be laying down quite detailed plans for the holiday period.

1 TUESDAY
Moon Age Day 14   Moon Sign Taurus

am . . . .

pm . . . .
Just discovering new possibilities could be pleasurable enough but right now you have scope to take things one stage further. You have what it takes to build on what you discover and to make others happier as a result. This might be a rather outlandish ambition, but it is part of what makes you who you are. Be prepared to seek support from friends.

2 WEDNESDAY
Moon Age Day 15   Moon Sign Gemini

am . . . .

pm . . . .
Today you can make use of extra vigour and work harder as a result. Make sure that what you are doing is going to benefit you later on because there isn't sufficient time to be going down blind alleys at the moment. The time is right to offer words of love to your partner, and practical help to anyone who has need of your very special skills.

3 THURSDAY
Moon Age Day 16   Moon Sign Gemini

am . . . .

pm . . . .
A much quieter and less demanding interlude is available as the Moon enters your solar fourth house. This also assists you to project yourself directly into the warmth of your family circle, where you can achieve real contentment. There is a little trepidation in the mind of some Pisceans, maybe regarding a possible confrontation later.

4 FRIDAY
Moon Age Day 17   Moon Sign Cancer

am . . . .

pm . . . .
In an emotional sense you might remain locked inside yourself, though
you needn't allow this to show practically if you insist to the world at
large that you are capable and very willing to get involved. Splitting your
nature in this way is not at all unusual for Pisces, and you are able to fool
anyone with your apparent confidence and dynamism.

5 SATURDAY
Moon Age Day 18   Moon Sign Cancer

am . . . .

pm . . . .
There is much to be said for seeking a little romance now and the signs
are very good when it comes to affairs of the heart. You can make this a
secure and happy sort of weekend, particularly if other people are doing
all they can to please you. Don't hold back when it comes to speaking
those important words that mean so much to others.

6 SUNDAY
Moon Age Day 19   Moon Sign Leo

am . . . .

pm . . . .
If you have anything to teach others at the moment – and chances are
you do – this is best achieved by example. Even when you lack some
confidence in your own abilities you needn't demonstrate the fact, and
should appear to be absolutely certain of everything. It's worth finishing
today on a social footing by getting together with good friends.

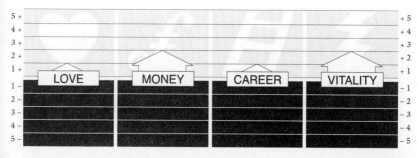

December 2009

YOUR MONTH AT A GLANCE

$\oplus$ = Opportunities are around   ⊖ = Be on the defensive   ○ = Life is pretty ordinary

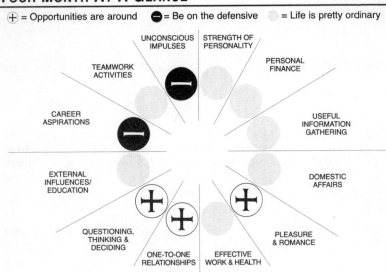

UNCONSCIOUS IMPULSES

STRENGTH OF PERSONALITY

TEAMWORK ACTIVITIES

PERSONAL FINANCE

CAREER ASPIRATIONS

USEFUL INFORMATION GATHERING

EXTERNAL INFLUENCES/ EDUCATION

DOMESTIC AFFAIRS

QUESTIONING, THINKING & DECIDING

PLEASURE & ROMANCE

ONE-TO-ONE RELATIONSHIPS

EFFECTIVE WORK & HEALTH

DECEMBER HIGHS AND LOWS

Here I show you how the rhythms of the Moon will affect you this month. Like the tide, your energies and abilities will rise and fall with its pattern. When it is above the centre line, go for it, when it is below, you should be resting.

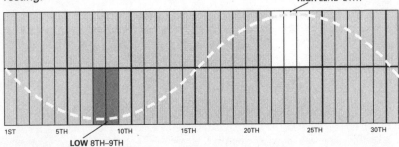

HIGH 22ND–24TH

LOW 8TH–9TH

1ST   5TH   10TH   15TH   20TH   25TH   30TH

7 MONDAY
Moon Age Day 20   Moon Sign Leo

am . . . .

pm . . . .
It could help today to pay attention to the finer details of life, especially where work is concerned. Don't worry if others aren't too keen on the way you present yourself – if you know it works, do it! You can't be flavour of the month with everyone at the moment, but should make the most of the fact that at least some people appreciate you.

8 TUESDAY
Moon Age Day 21   Moon Sign Virgo

am . . . .

pm . . . .
It's time to streamline your life and to focus only on what really matters. With the lunar low around you cannot afford to tackle too many jobs at the same time, even if there is an urge within you to feel as though something is being achieved. A little pretence may be necessary on those occasions when true confidence is lacking.

9 WEDNESDAY
Moon Age Day 22   Moon Sign Virgo

am . . . .

pm . . . .
The lunar low could encourage you to give way to some sloppy thinking, so it is worthwhile testing your ideas before you put them into practice. Don't be afraid to seek assistance if you need it, even if it means having to trawl around more than you really want to at the moment. Not the best day of the month – but keep trying!

10 THURSDAY
Moon Age Day 23   Moon Sign Libra

am . . . .

pm . . . .
You should now be in a better position for organising yourself at a practical level. Professional headway is easier to achieve and there are new and better incentives waiting in the wings. This could certainly be a favourable day as far as romance is concerned, particularly if you are willing to show your affection to a much greater extent.

11 FRIDAY

Moon Age Day 24   Moon Sign Libra

am . . . .

pm . . . .
There is only so much you can control today, so if you know in your heart
that you are trying to do too much, now is the time to slow things down.
It would be far better to do a couple of jobs well today than to do a
dozen things badly. Anything you can't address today can wait until later
in the month and could be better for the delay.

12 SATURDAY

Moon Age Day 25   Moon Sign Libra

am . . . .

pm . . . .
Socially speaking trends indicate a definite thirst for freedom and
excitement. Perhaps Pisces is developing the Christmas spirit already, and
this would not be particularly surprising because this is a time of year you
relish. Your best approach is to join in the fun wherever you find it and
arrange some sort of get-together yourself if possible.

13 SUNDAY

Moon Age Day 26   Moon Sign Scorpio

am . . . .

pm . . . .
There ought to be plenty of opportunity to expand your social horizons
and today offers newer and better opportunities for you to make a really
good impression all round. This is also an ideal time to plan your strategy
for the coming week, and to make certain everything is in place in terms
of your career.

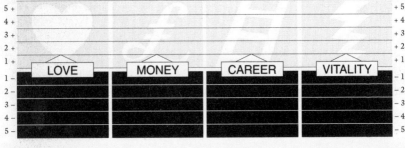

14 MONDAY   *Moon Age Day 27   Moon Sign Scorpio*

am . . . .

pm . . . .
You can get your own way today primarily through the use of your
charm, which is always the greatest weapon in the Piscean armoury. You
can put your talents to especially good use in a career setting and should
be on form when it comes to exploiting newer and better ideas. At home
you can now ensure that romance begins to blossom.

15 TUESDAY   *Moon Age Day 28   Moon Sign Sagittarius*

am . . . .

pm . . . .
In a professional sense you are now entering a more dynamic phase all
round, which might be something of a pity with Christmas just around
the corner. All the same you can make significant progress and should be
anxious to exploit your talents to the full. Routines could be a bit of bind,
especially if they prevent you from motoring on.

16 WEDNESDAY   *Moon Age Day 0   Moon Sign Sagittarius*

am . . . .

pm . . . .
Things could well be on a hair trigger when it comes to relationships, and
it's worth being especially careful not to offer unintended offence to
people who are too sensitive for their own good. This is less inclined to
happen at home, particularly if relationships there are settled and happy.
Be ready to address the needs of friends.

17 THURSDAY   *Moon Age Day 1   Moon Sign Capricorn*

am . . . .

pm . . . .
You will have a sense of being virtually driven by your need to exploit
new opportunities in your life and because of this you might not be
giving as much attention as usual to the impending festivities. Social
events could change your attitude, particularly if you are willing to be the
life and soul of just about any party around now.

18 FRIDAY   *Moon Age Day 2   Moon Sign Capricorn*

am . . . .

pm . . . .
You can keep things moving forward under present astrological trends and there is no sign of life slowing down at any time now. On the contrary, you may be burning the candle at both ends and that could mean fatigue unless you are careful. Who knows where new possibilities will lead? Life should be very exciting.

19 SATURDAY   *Moon Age Day 3   Moon Sign Capricorn*

am . . . .

pm . . . .
Even if you continue to show your best and most organised face to the world, you could stumble when you come across anyone who doesn't respond to your charm. There are always going to be those who are immune to your delightful personality but in the rush to achieve even greater success you may simply have to ignore them.

20 SUNDAY   *Moon Age Day 4   Moon Sign Aquarius*

am . . . .

pm . . . .
Mars is now in your solar sixth house, assisting you to show greater and greater effectiveness when it matters the most. If anything, you might be slightly hampered by the fact that you can't do anything too practical on a Sunday. At the same time, getting into Christmas mode with others can make all the difference.

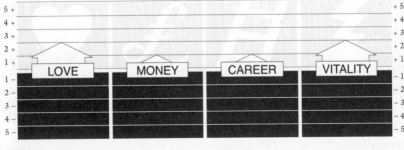

21 MONDAY
Moon Age Day 5   Moon Sign Aquarius

am . . . .

pm . . . .
Getting your own way remains generally simple and is down to a combination of determination and your naturally winning ways. It's all about knowing that what you believe is right, and when you have true conviction on your side you are unlikely to be stopped. Social moments could be quieter, but a romantic interlude is still possible.

22 TUESDAY
Moon Age Day 6   Moon Sign Pisces

am . . . .

pm . . . .
Continuing to succeed and to move forward is simply a matter of being in the right place at the most opportune time. The lunar high should help you to take care of this and to reach a better understanding of what to do next. Everything now is about moving forward, and you probably won't take at all kindly to any sort of interruption.

23 WEDNESDAY
Moon Age Day 7   Moon Sign Pisces

am . . . .

pm . . . .
If you have been fairly well occupied, you may have more or less forgotten that Christmas is just two days away. Use the power of the lunar high to get any remaining shopping done and to help you to find some bargains. Good luck may also on your side in other ways. Prepare to make last-minute changes work to your advantage.

24 THURSDAY
Moon Age Day 8   Moon Sign Pisces

am . . . .

pm . . . .
The lunar high still lingers around you during Christmas Eve, which offers an extra boost in terms of energy and general happiness. You have what it takes to get things to drop into place at present and to give life the odd nudge in the right direction if necessary. Time alone with someone you love would be no bad thing this evening.

25 FRIDAY

Moon Age Day 9   Moon Sign Aries

am . . . .

pm . . . .
You have potential to be at your happiest for Christmas Day if you
surround yourself with people who are extremely important to you.
Strangers take a back seat, even if you are out of the house and
socialising. From a romantic point of view today could prove to be quite
unique and some Pisceans could be in for a very special surprise.

26 SATURDAY

Moon Age Day 10   Moon Sign Aries

am . . . .

pm . . . .
Your lively, friendly attitude to the world at large means you may not be
too keen to be trapped in the same place today – even if that is your own
comfortable home. This would be an ideal time to visit relatives and to
look out friends you don't get to see as much as you would wish. Stand
by for a rollicking knees-up by the evening!

27 SUNDAY

Moon Age Day 11   Moon Sign Taurus

am . . . .

pm . . . .
You seem to get the very best from communicating today. This is because
you have what it takes to modify your own nature for the sake of those
around you. You can get even the most difficult of individuals to once
again fall prey to your charm, and have what it takes to deal effectively
with all practical matters. Don't forget to save time for your partner.

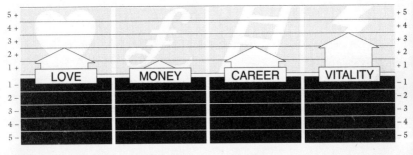

28 MONDAY

Moon Age Day 12   Moon Sign Taurus

am . . . .

pm . . . .
Any new social contacts you make should offer a marvellous tonic because just at the moment Pisces is as gregarious and sociable as it ever gets. Whilst others might get tired of the social whirl and demand a little rest, you can afford to dance on until dawn. If anyone can make the best of the Christmas holidays, you will probably be one of them.

29 TUESDAY

Moon Age Day 13   Moon Sign Taurus

am . . . .

pm . . . .
You have a talent for working hard and effectively, and can really show this now. Some Pisceans will be back at work and if you are one of them it's worth making certain that superiors know that you are around. There is nothing at all wrong with singing your own praises a little today, particularly if there is less competition around for the moment.

30 WEDNESDAY

Moon Age Day 14   Moon Sign Gemini

am . . . .

pm . . . .
A fresh exchange of views should suit you fine today, and you needn't be at all insulted if someone wishes to modify one of your own notions. You are great when it comes to co-operation – even with people who have been difficult to deal with in the past. Niggling routines could get in the way of absolute enjoyment within your home.

31 THURSDAY

Moon Age Day 15   Moon Sign Gemini

am . . . .

pm . . . .
New Year's Eve could not fall at a better time for you in an astrological sense. The position of Venus in particular assists you in large groups and ensures that your party spirit is still burning brightly. You have every reason to exit the year with a great sense of optimism. You also have exactly what it takes to be extremely helpful.

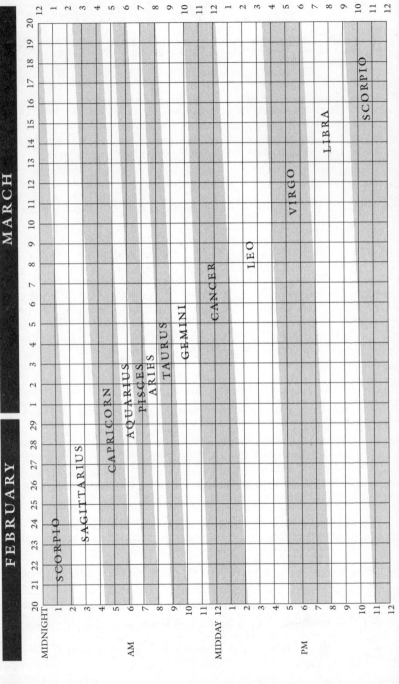

THE ZODIAC, PLANETS AND CORRESPONDENCES

The Earth revolves around the Sun once every calendar year, so when viewed from Earth the Sun appears in a different part of the sky as the year progresses. In astrology, these parts of the sky are divided into the signs of the zodiac and this means that the signs are organised in a circle. The circle begins with Aries and ends with Pisces.

Taking the zodiac sign as a starting point, astrologers then work with all the positions of planets, stars and many other factors to calculate horoscopes and birth charts and tell us what the stars have in store for us.

The table below shows the planets and Elements for each of the signs of the zodiac. Each sign belongs to one of the four Elements: Fire, Air, Earth or Water. Fire signs are creative and enthusiastic; Air signs are mentally active and thoughtful; Earth signs are constructive and practical; Water signs are emotional and have strong feelings.

It also shows the metals and gemstones associated with, or corresponding with, each sign. The correspondence is made when a metal or stone possesses properties that are held in common with a particular sign of the zodiac.

Finally, the table shows the opposite of each star sign – this is the opposite sign in the astrological circle.

Placed	Sign	Symbol	Element	Planet	Metal	Stone	Opposite
1	Aries	Ram	Fire	Mars	Iron	Bloodstone	Libra
2	Taurus	Bull	Earth	Venus	Copper	Sapphire	Scorpio
3	Gemini	Twins	Air	Mercury	Mercury	Tiger's Eye	Sagittarius
4	Cancer	Crab	Water	Moon	Silver	Pearl	Capricorn
5	Leo	Lion	Fire	Sun	Gold	Ruby	Aquarius
6	Virgo	Maiden	Earth	Mercury	Mercury	Sardonyx	Pisces
7	Libra	Scales	Air	Venus	Copper	Sapphire	Aries
8	Scorpio	Scorpion	Water	Pluto	Plutonium	Jasper	Taurus
9	Sagittarius	Archer	Fire	Jupiter	Tin	Topaz	Gemini
10	Capricorn	Goat	Earth	Saturn	Lead	Black Onyx	Cancer
11	Aquarius	Waterbearer	Air	Uranus	Uranium	Amethyst	Leo
12	Pisces	Fishes	Water	Neptune	Tin	Moonstone	Virgo

Foulsham books can be found in all
good bookshops or direct from
www.foulsham.com